The Man Who Fed the World

The Man Who Fed the World

Nobel Peace Prize Laureate Norman Borlaug and His Battle to End World Hunger

An Authorized Biography

By Leon Hesser

Foreword by Jimmy Carter

Copyright © 2009, Leon Hesser, all rights reserved.

No part of this book may be reproduced in any form or by any electronic or mechanical means, including information storage and retrieval systems, without written permission in writing from the publisher, except by reviewers, who may quote brief passages in a review.

Printed in the United States of America

For Information:
Righter's Mill Press LLC
475 Wall Street
Princeton, NJ 08540

Library of Congress Cataloging-in-Publication Data
Hesser, Leon, 1925

The Man Who Fed the World/ Leon Hesser

Library of Congress Counted Number 2008941721

ISBN 978-1-948460-10-1

Second Edition

Visit our website: http://www.rightersmill.com

R0458406288

Books by the same author

Nurture the Heart, Feed the World: The inspiring life journeys of two vagabonds. Austin: Synergy Books (2004).

The Taming of the Wilderness: Indiana's Transition from Indian Hunting Grounds to Hoosier Farmland: 1800-1875. Bloomington: AuthorHouse (2002).

Contents

Foreword

The title of this biography, *The Man Who Fed the World*, is indeed appropriate. My good friend Norman Borlaug has accomplished more than any other one individual in history in the battle to end world hunger.

As a young Rockefeller Foundation scientist in the mid-20th century, Dr. Borlaug developed high-yielding varieties of wheat that took Mexico from near-starvation to self-sufficiency within a few years. A decade later, when India and Pakistan suffered widespread hunger and even famine, he introduced his new seed and production technologies in the Asian sub-continent and successfully campaigned at the highest levels of government to get policy changes that averted famine in the mid to late 1960s. In response to the combination of his scientific and humanitarian achievements, the Nobel Committee awarded Dr. Borlaug the Nobel Peace Prize in 1970.

That was only the beginning of his remarkable accomplishments. Since 1970, for example, Norman Borlaug has made a number of trips to China, where his technology, his policy suggestions, and his training of young Chinese scientists helped alleviate hunger in that country of 1.3 billion people. In the Southern Cone of South America, the early maturity of his Mexican wheats permitted double cropping of wheat and soybeans, with tremendous increases in production. For his technology and his humanitarian efforts, he is revered in many countries throughout Asia, the Middle East, Latin America, and Africa.

Since 1986, I have had the distinct pleasure of working with Norman Borlaug in sub-Saharan Africa where, in spite of AIDS, endemic malaria and other maladies, populations are increasing faster than food supplies. I have witnessed first-hand the reverence that thousands upon thousands of Africans have for Dr. Borlaug's untiring efforts to relieve their hunger.

Norman Borlaug's scientific achievements have saved hundreds of millions of lives and earned him the distinction as one of the 100 most influential individuals of the 20th century. I commend Leon Hesser for making more people aware of the remarkable life and achievements of this American hero.

Jimmy Carter

Preface

Norman Borlaug was the only person during the twentieth century who was awarded the Nobel Peace Prize for work in agriculture and food. There is no Nobel Food Prize, so the Nobel Committee chose Dr. Borlaug as the 1970 recipient of the Peace Prize based on his dramatic scientific breakthroughs and wheat production technology that relieved hunger in much of the world. During the previous decade, many people on the planet Earth, most notably in China and the Asian Subcontinent, were facing starvation, even famine. Borlaug's revolutionary achievements relieved widespread human suffering and brought peace.

Today, Dr. Borlaug is hailed as the person who saved the lives of more people—hundreds of millions—from starvation than any person in history. He earned the distinction as one of the 100 most influential individuals of the 20th century. His is an inspiring story; he has gone from an unpretentious Iowa farm boy to scientist-cum-humanist of world acclaim.

What is it that made Norman Borlaug different? What drove him? What can we—especially our youth—learn from his life? My objective in writing his biography is to shed light on those questions.

Norman Borlaug and I first met in Pakistan in 1966. I was Foreign Service Officer in charge of US efforts to increase the country's food production. My team of technical advisors taught Pakistan's agricultural extension staff to train farmers in the proper techniques for cultivating Borlaug's high-yielding varieties of wheat to obtain previously unheard-of yields. In the early to mid-1960s, even while importing millions of tons of donated food grains from the US, Canada and Australia, Pakistan was on the verge of starvation. Based on Borlaug's "miracle" wheats as the catalyst, Pakistan doubled wheat production and achieved self-sufficiency in food grains by 1968.

A comparable program using Borlaug's wheat seeds and associated technology in India, where starvation had turned to famine in parts of the country in the mid-1960s, resulted in a "wheat revolution" that, together with similar efforts for rice, brought the country to self-sufficiency in wheat in 1972 and in all cereals by 1974.

Writing the life story of this great man is one of the most rewarding things I have ever done. A highlight of the experience was four days that I spent in June 2005 with Norman and his remarkable family at their home in Dallas, Texas. His wife, Margaret, whom I had not met before, is every bit Norman's equal in terms of spunk and spirit. Daughter Jeanie, son Bill, their children and grandchildren all exhibit traits that stem from strong genes. And it is clearly apparent that they all have the deepest admiration for both Norman and Margaret. A remarkable family, indeed.

Norman Borlaug still uses varied means to bring his influence to bear on public policy—at home as well as abroad. He is a much-sought-after public speaker. In recent years, he has testified before congressional committees; spoken to audiences of all political ideologies around the world, often on occasions when he received yet another of his fifty-plus honorary degrees; and been a frequent contributor to op-ed pieces in influential publications such as the *New York Times* and the *Wall Street Journal.*

In a collaborative effort with former US President Jimmy

Carter, Dr. Borlaug continues his quest against hunger; he makes a few trips each year to Africa to help solve food problems south of the Sahara. He had just recently returned from one of those trips when he called me from his base in Mexico on March 26, 2004 and said, "Leon, I didn't get much work done yesterday. It was hectic around here. They celebrated my 90th birthday!"

Leon Hesser
Naples, Florida
September 2005

Dear Friends:

Throughout this book, Leon Hesser introduces some of the people who have had profound influences on my life. To each of them, as well as to the many, many colleagues, scientists and associates with whom I have worked throughout the years, I am grateful.

Above all, I owe deep gratitude to my family for tolerating the habits of their vagabond husband and father as he carried on his work in distant corners of the Earth. Without their steadfast support, I would have faltered.

My overarching dream is that the life story that Leon Hesser has herewith chronicled will serve as an inspiration to young people to devote thought, energy and focused effort toward scientific and allied pursuits aimed at alleviating hunger and poverty throughout the world.

With all best wishes,

Norman E. Borlaug

The Man Who Fed the World

Chapter One

Growing Up on an Iowa Farm

"Give the best that God gave you. If you won't do that, don't bother to compete."

—David Bartelma,
high-school principal and coach

A string of phone calls came from Oslo, Norway, early in the morning—before daybreak—on October 20, 1970: "Could I speak with Dr. Borlaug, please? I have an urgent message."

Margaret took the first eight calls: "I'm sorry, but my husband has already gone to work in the field. Could I take a message?"

"No, madam. I need to speak with him personally. It's an important matter, strictly private."

Finally, on the sixth call, the person on the other end said, "I'm a reporter from the Oslo newspaper, *Aftenposten*; I really need to speak with Dr. Borlaug. You see, the Chairman of the Nobel Selection Committee is to announce at 2:00 p.m. today, Oslo time—three hours from now—that your husband has been awarded the Nobel Peace Prize. How can we get in touch with him?"

Margaret was awestruck. She thought, *How could that be? The message is not from the Nobel Foundation—maybe it's some kind of hoax.*

After taking two more calls and asking questions, she was convinced that the callers were serious. She must get word to Norman.

She called the project office in Mexico City. A car and driver would pick her up in 30 minutes to take her to the Toluca Agricultural Experiment Station. She took the phone off the hook as she dressed for the trip.

Toluca was thirty miles away; the last eight miles were over bad, muddy roads. It seemed to take forever. As they traveled along, Margaret wondered what Norman's reaction would be. Would he be skeptical? Elated? Dumbfounded? What if it really were a hoax?

When they arrived at Toluca, Margaret scurried to the ramshackle hacienda, "headquarters" of the experiment station, and quickly looked around for Norman. He wasn't there. In her "kitchen Spanish," she asked where she might find her husband.

"But, *Senora, el doctor* is at the far end of the station. It's too far to walk, and it's very difficult to get there by car."

"Oh my, it's terribly important that I see him. I have an urgent message."

Noting that Margaret was distraught, the station manager arranged for one of his drivers to take her in a pick-up truck. She found Norman working with six young scientists—two Romanians, one Brazilian, one American and two Mexicans—all in sweaty, mud-stained clothes. Within the next five or six days, they had to make eight thousand individual selections of wheat plants, thresh and pack the grain, and get the seeds to the Sonora experiment station by November 1 for planting in the winter nursery.

Norm was puzzled when he saw the pick-up coming his way, but he remained bent over and kept on with his work. He was startled when he saw that it was Margaret. He rushed over and kissed her. He sensed that she was excited. Her heart was beating rapidly. Then he said, "What in heaven's name brings you out here? Has something happened to Dad, or Mother?"

"Norman, you've been awarded the Nobel Peace Prize. I had a string of phone calls this morning from reporters of the Oslo newspaper, *Aftenposten,* confirming it."

Norm looked astonished. Then, in disbelief, he said, "No. No. That can't be, Margaret. Someone's pulling your leg." He went back to selecting wheat plants.

While Margaret was trying to convince Norm that the news was true, another pick-up truck came toward them—carrying six reporters with their cameras. Word had reached the Mexico City press.

The lives of Norman and Margaret Borlaug would never be the same. . .

From the day he was born in 1914, Norman Borlaug has been an enigma. How could a child of the Iowa prairie, who attended a one-teacher, one-room school; who flunked the university entrance exam; and whose highest ambition was to be a high school science teacher and athletic coach, ultimately achieve the distinction as one of the one hundred most influential persons of the twentieth century? And receive the Nobel Peace Prize for averting hunger and famine? And eventually be hailed as the man who saved hundreds of millions of lives from starvation—more than any other person in history?

It all started in the small Norwegian-American community of Saude, in an area known as "Little Norway," near the county-seat town of Cresco—population 3,500—in northeastern Iowa, about fifteen miles from the Minnesota state line. All four of Norman's grandparents were of mid-nineteenth century Norwegian immigrant families. All were bilingual. The Norwegian language was commonly heard in Little Norway until well into the twentieth century.

Norman is proud of his heritage. From his family and neighbors in the counties Howard and Chickasaw, he absorbed early on many traits that served him well throughout his life. Norm says, "I learned to know right from wrong from my parents, grandparents and neighbors."

Until Norman was eight, he and his parents—Henry and Clara Vaala Borlaug—lived with his grandparents, Nels and Emma Borlaug, on their 120 acre farm. Living together as an extended family was common among the early Norwegian immigrants in rural Iowa. With that proximity, Grandfather Nels was to have a marked influence on Norman's life. Norm says, "Grandfather Nels was very special to me while I was growing up. He often took me with him to go fishing. As we would sit together on the banks of Little Turkey River, waiting for a nibble, he would explain how important it was to help other people in times of need. In his distinct Norwegian accent, he would say, 'Norm-boy, your good deeds will be returned in ways you can never imagine.' "

In 1854, Nels Borlaug's parents, Ole and Solveig Borlaug, had sailed across the Atlantic with a group of other Norwegian families. They were concerned about the upheaval in Europe, fraught with hunger caused by the late-blight potato famine during 1845 to 1850, and faced with privation due to the continent's population increasing faster than food production. The Borlaugs were struggling farmers on a 150-meter strip of poor land that stretched along Norway's Sogn Fjord. They depended to a large extent on fish and potatoes for food. In America, they would look for land with fertile soil, where they could start a new life.

Crossing the Atlantic was challenging for emigrants in the

mid-nineteenth century. By then a few steamships were plying between Europe and America and they could cross in half the time required for sailing ships, which typically took four to six weeks. But the Borlaugs came the slower way—by sailing vessels—because that was much cheaper, though certainly less comfortable. The Borlaug family and their fellow passengers came up the St. Lawrence and settled at Norway Grove, Dane County, Wisconsin, where Nels Borlaug was born on October 25, 1859.[1] Five or six years later, the Borlaugs settled in northeast Iowa near the village of Saude.

Saude had been established by Norwegian immigrant families, including the Vaalas, the Landsverks, and the Swenumsons, all of whom had sailed on the same ship from Saude, Telemark, Norway in 1848. The families had a close, interdependent bond and soon began to intermarry. The Vaalas and the Landsverks were Norman's mother's paternal grandparents. The Swenumsons and the Borlaugs were Norman's father's grandparents.

The small community joined together and built a wooden church that all the neighbors attended and supported. The Borlaugs, who were Lutherans, attended every Sunday. Norman recalls that when he was a child, the pastor gave two sermons at the church each Sunday morning—one in Norwegian and one in English.

Norman's Grandfather Nels, the third son of Ole and Solveig Borlaug, attended school for only three years, until he could read, write and figure. That was typical for farm families of the day. But he was left with a deep hunger for the education that circumstances had denied him.

When Nels came of age, he courted and married Emma Swenumson. Nels and Emma had three sons and a daughter. Henry, the second son, was Norman's father. Nels was determined that his children should get a better formal education than he had had, and they all did.

Norman's father, Henry, is the middle son of Nels and Emma Borlaug.

Henry was a quiet, studious person, interested especially in history and agricultural subjects. He went to the same small school that his father had attended, but for all eight grades. He then attended two winter sessions at a nearby business school, where he met and fell in love with Clara Vaala. The two young people married and settled in with Nels and Emma Borlaug.

A large wood-fired heater kept the Borlaug house warm in

winter, and the daily bread was baked in a wood-fired oven in the kitchen. On the farm was an old log cabin where Nels had lived as a boy. Later the old log structure served as a tool shed and a place to store oat seed. Corn seed was stored in the house, to avoid damage by mice and rats.

Norm recalls from stories handed down by Grandfather Nels that the Borlaugs and their Bohemian neighbors were duly impressed when the famous Czech composer Antonin Dvorak was visiting nearby. Dvorak spent the summer of 1893 with friends in Spillville, Iowa, a flourishing community of Bohemians just thirteen miles from the Borlaug farm. While there, Dvorak composed the "American" string quartet, found the inspiration for *Humoresque*, and finished his popular Ninth Symphony, known as *The New World Symphony*. Norm says, "He came to Spillville because he wanted to get a flavor of Bohemian America. People in Howard County knew Dvorak was in Spillville; they talked about it a lot." Later, a graveled road—called the Dvorak highway—ran from Cresco through Protivin to Spillville. A park in Spillville is named in Dvorak's honor. *The New World Symphony* premiered in New York in December 1893.

"Common sense" was one of the cardinal rules in the Borlaug family. Hard work was another. Norman developed his work ethic at an early age. He worked in the fields and helped care for the livestock. Crops on the Borlaug homestead were mainly corn, oats, and clover. The clover served as pasture for the cows and horses during the summer and was made into hay for winter feeding. Corn and oats fattened pigs and steers for market. A couple of the fattest pigs and a steer were kept to butcher during the winter.

A hand-cranked separator divided the milk from the farm's dairy cows into cream and skimmed milk. The cream was sold through the Saude Cooperative Creamery, which processed it into butter that was shipped to Chicago. The skimmed milk was fed to the pigs. Eggs from a flock of chickens were traded for merchandise—mainly wheat flour, sugar and coffee—at the Saude general store.

One time during his first year in school, Norman begged to stay home and work, but his Grandfather Nels said, "Norm-boy, it's better to fill your head now if you want to fill your belly later." Old Nels constantly counseled his grandson with phrases like, "Education and common sense, thinking things out for yourself—that's what matters. Get yourself a good education. No one can take that away from you."

When Norman was eight, he and his parents moved to a farm that his father had bought adjoining Grandfather Nels' land. Nels spent much time with the boy. Each autumn, Norm, his father and Grandfather Nels would go squirrel and rabbit hunting together. Norm's mother would prepare and bake the meat for supper.

Grandfather Nels practiced his own type of religion, seven days a week. He had no use for the habits of people who went to church on Sunday but whose morals were lax the rest of the time. Old Nels would frequently say to Norm, "Some people look up in the sky in search of God. I say, look at the soil and the growing things. That's where you'll find God."

Norm started to school when he was five years old, walking a mile and a half each way. For comfort and protection, especially during winter, older neighborhood children accompanied him. As he grew older he in turn walked his two sisters to school—Palma, two years younger, and Charlotte, five years younger. If a severe snow blizzard arose, his father or a neighbor with children in the school would hitch horses to a sled and come get them; otherwise they walked.

Norm's first eight grades of school were in the same one-teacher, one-room schoolhouse—New Oregon Township # 8—

New Oregon Township School # 8.

that his father and grandfather had attended. Writing paper was scarce, so the students wrote their lessons with chalk on slate. Norm says, "We did our numbers on the blackboard." Teachers came and went on a yearly basis. A pot-bellied, wood-burning stove heated the school. Two toilets, one for the girls and one for the boys, were outside. Little had changed since his father and grandfather had studied there.

In reflecting on his childhood, Norm says, "The environment in our own home was excellent. Everyone was kind, quiet and considerate. There never was any quarreling. My mother was a small woman. She was very shy. She was a good mother, an excellent cook, and a wonderful seamstress. Palma and Charlotte always looked nice in dresses home-sewn by Mother. Mother loved to bake bread, cakes and pies; they were delicious. My sisters and I would go back to the woods on our farm and gather wild blackberries, raspberries and cherries for her. In the fall, she would preserve food for the winter by canning it in glass jars: corn, beets, peas, carrots, black currents, gooseberries, rhubarb, and even chicken.

"My father was a tall man—about six feet one inch. He

worked incredibly long hours in the field—from sun-up to sundown—during the spring, summer and fall. But he also loved to read—the daily newspapers, journals, and magazines, especially *Wallace's Farmer* and *National Geographic*, all delivered by Rural Free Delivery to mail boxes a half mile from the farm. During a winter evening, Dad would often read a chapter of a book to us children."

The Borlaugs were a close-knit family. Norm says, "All the Borlaugs—uncles, aunts and cousins—would get together one Sunday each month for dinner, and also on the main holidays. Granddad played the accordion and violin, and the whole family would join in and sing. On Christmas, Thanksgiving and the Fourth of July, Granddad Nels always gave each of us twelve grandchildren a silver dollar—he didn't like paper money!"

"Life on the farm was austere," Norm says. "We had to be frugal. We were poor in material things, but we never went hungry. We were always well-clothed, both winter and summer. We always had home-baked bread, lots of eggs, and plenty of milk and butter from the cows. We had plenty of potatoes from Granddad's potato patch, which was his pride and joy. We had apples from the orchard that Granddad had planted, and all kinds of berries. Mostly, we enjoyed life. We sang both English and Norwegian songs that we learned from our parents and grandparents. Dad and I even sang while we hand-milked our fifteen cows."

Threshing—separating the ripened oat grain from the straw—was a community affair in Little Norway during July and August. Norm says, "When I was a boy, the community had a large threshing circle that included twenty to thirty farms. A steam engine powered the separator—a large threshing machine that separated the grain from the straw."

Later, Norm's Uncle Ned Borlaug owned a smaller threshing machine, powered by a Fordson tractor, which served a smaller group of neighboring farms in the Saude community. Uncle

Ned's son, Arthur, who is four years younger than Norm, described the process to me and explained how Norm helped with the threshing during the summers. The "ring" consisted of about fifteen neighboring farmers. The group went from one farm to the next, threshing oats. With horse-drawn wagons, the farmers transported oat bundles from the field to the threshing machine in the barn lot. In turn, each would pitch his bundles into the thresher. Arthur said, "Norm's job was to operate the grain elevator, powered by a one-cylinder Fairbanks Morse gasoline engine, which conveyed the threshed oats into the host farmer's grain bin. When the threshing was finished on one farm, Norm moved the grain elevator to the next farm with a team of horses."

The threshing ring also served an important social function. The neighborhood women moved from farm to farm with the crew and prepared large noontime dinners, complete with pies and cakes, for their hungry men.

During Norman's final year in the rural school, the family decided that he should go to high school, which was unusual in rural Iowa at the time, especially for boys. A cousin, Sina Borlaug, had been his teacher during his last couple of years in the one-room school and encouraged the family to make sure he pursued his education. She said, "He's no great shakes as a scholar; his arithmetic is awful—but he sticks to it. He's got grit! High school will make him."

The Borlaug farm was fourteen miles from the high school in Cresco. There were no school buses. Six boys in the neighborhood took turns driving their family's Model T Ford to take them to Cresco, leaving at seven in the morning for nine o'clock classes. They left after classes at four in the afternoon to drive back home before dark. Norm says, "The commuting made it difficult for us to compete in extra-curricular activities; football practice was impossible for my first two years."

At high school, Norm's classes were oriented toward agriculture. Rather than preparing young people for college, the courses were looked at as preparation for boys to go back and work on the farms. Even then, the vocational agriculture teacher—Harry Schroeder, a recent graduate of Iowa State College—sensed that Norman had a keen mind and had an innate curiosity about the processes of plant growth and the nature of soils. Norm says, "Under Mr. Schroeder's direction, our crops class set up one of the first on-farm chemical fertilizer tests on hybrid corn in Howard County."

Norm's sister Palma said, "Norman was always asking questions; he had a curious mind. Growing things fascinated him from his childhood. He always had a feeling for plants, a passionate desire to know how they grew. He was curious about the change of seasons and the migrations of wild ducks and geese. He would ask, 'Why do the other birds—robins, blackbirds, bobolinks—not migrate in flocks, like ducks and geese? And why do the weasel and jackrabbit change their brown coats to white?' "

Perhaps the most influential person during Norm's high school days was David Bartelma. In addition to being Cresco High's principal, he was the athletic coach. In 1924, he had gone to the Olympic Games as an alternate on the American wresting team. Norm's toughness and courage had brought him to Bartelma's attention. Bartelma convinced Norman to join the school's wrestling squad. Norm became one of the school's best athletes—a champion wrestler and a star football and baseball player.

Bartelma's challenge to Norman was, "Give the best that God gave you. If you won't do that, don't bother to compete." He had given his young athlete a code for life.

In late October 1929, during Norm's first year in high school, the New York stock market crashed. Even for a decade before that, farm states had been in a depression. At the end of World War I, the bottom fell out of agricultural prices. Many farmers, unable to make payments on mortgages, lost their farms. Between 1920 and 1933, one farm in every four was sold for debts or taxes. The Borlaugs saw hard times, too, due to the low prices for their produce, but because they had no debt they fared better than most. Norm's father, Grandfather Nels, and Uncle Oscar worked their farms as one unit. Norm credits his father and Uncle Oscar with saving the farm business. Norm says, "When we built new buildings on Dad's place in 1922, we did not build a barn because Dad didn't have the money and he refused to go into debt. He managed for seven years with a long, makeshift stable for the cows and horses."

Norm recalls, "Uncle Oscar was a self-made economist. He read a lot of university books on economics—textbooks used at Cornell University, for example. I would overhear family discussions in which Oscar would say to Granddad, Uncle Ned and my dad, whom they called Hank, 'This bubble is going to collapse. Hank, get your money out of the bank and build a barn.' Dad listened. He had bought and paid for lumber to build a barn just two months before the crash of '29. Then when the bubble broke, Oscar said, 'I told you so!' "

When Norm graduated from Cresco High, he was given the Legion Citizenship Award at commencement for his demonstrated courage, character, service and scholarship. He also received the coach's Athletic Medal. But he had to face the harsh realities of a deepening depression in the economy. He decided to lay out a year before going to college, to save some money. He cut oak fence posts for thirty-five cents a day; during the busy harvest season he hired out to neighbors for a dollar a day. He hunted and trapped for muskrat, skunk and mink in the snowy woods during the winter, checking his traps early each morning. He sold most of the pelts for a few cents each, and the meat from some of the trapped animals served the family as food. He says, "Once in 1933 I caught a beautiful, dark mink. I got $10 for the pelt. That was a lot of money!"

Despite the economic deprivations, Grandfather Nels, who recognized that Norman was always curious and had a quick mind, encouraged his grandson to go to college. "Get a university education. Get there, Norm-boy, any way you can."

By early summer 1933, Norm had saved nearly $60. His father offered to double the amount if he enrolled in a university. Norman argued that father's money should be used for the education of his sisters, Palma and Charlotte. "I can work and pay my own way; they cannot."

Norman's high-school graduation picture.

Chapter Two

A Budding Scientist at the University of Minnesota

"I proceeded to flunk the entrance exam beautifully."
—Norman Borlaug

George Champlin, a buddy who had graduated from Cresco High a few years before Norman, was a running back on the University of Minnesota football squad. He tried to persuade Norman to go with him to Minneapolis and enroll in the University of Minnesota. Norm wasn't sure that was the right thing for him. He was planning to go to Iowa State Teachers College, where he had the promise of a job for which his food would be the pay. Norm says, "My ambition was to be a high-school science teacher and coach."

Champlin said, "Norman, I'm leaving tomorrow for early football practice. I'll drive you up to the twin cities. We'll find you a job and a place to live. If it turns out you don't like it up there, you can hitchhike back to Iowa in time to start at Teachers College."

With that, Norm agreed to go with Champlin. Grandfather Nels was thrilled. Before the boys drove away, Nels, who had no use for paper money, reached in his pocket and gave Norman eleven silver dollars. He said, "You'll make more use of 'em than I will, Norm-boy."

Norm now had a little more than $70 to start his academic career. Tuition fees for the first quarter would be $25, which would leave only about $45 for rent and food. But Champlin said, "We'll get you a job for your meals, and for a dollar a week you can share my apartment."

Norm considered himself lucky. He got a job right away at the University Coffee Shop: "Work an hour, get a meal—three times a day." That was the pay. Norm recalls that breakfast at the beanery consisted of a dish of prunes, two slices of toast, and coffee.

One morning shortly after he started at the coffee shop, as he sat down for breakfast, Norm noticed a pretty girl opposite him. Their eyes met, she smiled, and they struck up a conversation. "My name is Margaret Gibson. I'm a sophomore in the College of Education. What are you studying?"

Margaret Gibson Borlaug

Slightly embarrassed, Norman said, "I don't know yet, I just got here and I haven't registered."

The quiet farm boy was spellbound by Margaret's friendly, open manner, her engaging conversation, her sculptured face, her shiny black hair. She was very attractive.

As she spoke in a sophisticated, low, cool voice Norm learned that Margaret had two brothers, George and Francis, who had studied at the University of Minnesota and had encouraged her to go there. Both brothers had played varsity football. In 1929, George had been an All-American guard and captain. Margaret also had a sister and two other brothers. Despite having no wealth and few possessions, the family was a contented one and Margaret had grown up feeling secure and optimistic.

Margaret told Norm that she earned her room and board by waiting tables, babysitting, and doing other odd jobs during the evenings.

Margaret was attracted to the shy farm boy from Iowa.

Norm was pleased that Margaret had engaged him in conversation. He looked forward to seeing her again soon.

Norm was fascinated and also disturbed by what he observed in the twin cities. Minneapolis and St. Paul had a total population of nearly three-quarters of a million. As he explored the city he was troubled by the evidence of human misery, the likes of which he had never seen before. He pondered: "Back on the farm, despite the Depression, bank failures and farm foreclosures, we nearly always had plenty of food. But here in the city where people depend on a cash economy there is both hunger for food and hunger for work." Hundreds of unemployed were begging for a nickel to buy bread and were sleeping on the ground in the parks.

So many people were caught in the depths of the Depression. Those images were to stay with Norman and cause him to be determined—somehow—to do what he could to improve the lot of fellow human beings.

During his second week in the city, Norman took the university streetcar to visit the agriculture campus in St. Paul, about five miles from the main campus. He liked the "farm campus" and resolved to try to enroll in the College of Agriculture.

Borlaug lacked a solid academic background for university studies, not because of any shortage of innate ability, but because of his limited opportunities at home. A one-room, one-teacher grammar school was hardly sufficient preparation for higher education. And Iowa's high schools at that time, at best, were rated as one year short of the standards for Minnesota's schools, lagging in both science and mathematics. For that reason, aspiring students from out of state were required to take an entrance examination to assess their academic potential.

Mark G. Yudof, a president of the university fifty years later, said, "When Norman Borlaug came to the University of Minnesota as a student in 1933, his ability to do university work was questioned."

In fact, he failed the entrance exam.

"But today," President Yudof declared, "we are proud to have named a building in his honor. Dr. Borlaug's life story should be an inspiration to everyone."

Norm was depressed when he didn't pass the entrance exam. But there was another option. That year, for the first time, applicants who did not meet the entrance standards for the university could be admitted to the new General College, which the university had opened to serve a "different though not inferior" student.

General College students were made aware of culture through music appreciation, which included Gershwin as well as Bach and Beethoven. They studied the history of drama. In English they read Shakespeare and Charlie Chan stories. A writing laboratory was introduced where students could come in at their leisure and write class notes, reports for other subjects, short stories, essays —even letters home—and get assistance where needed. There were survey courses in world history, economics, biology, chemistry, and mathematics.[2]

In offering Borlaug admittance to the General College, the dean said, "If you do well you can earn an associate's degree in two years."

This was far short of Norman's goal—and of the aspirations that his grandfather had instilled in him.

That evening Norman and Margaret ate together in the coffee shop. Norm was more than discouraged; he was despondent. He spilled out his frustration as he walked her home for the first time. "I know I'm nothing special, but I know damn well I'm better than that!"

Margaret was sympathetic and tried to encourage him. "This could be a chance to broaden your general education." She was flattered that Norman had confided in her. Over the years, Margaret gradually became aware of how deeply Norman felt about the academic rejection.

But Borlaug turned his rancor into determination. He worked hard at the General College and made decent grades. Toward the end of his second quarter, he mustered the courage to go see Dr. Fred Hovde, who was assistant director of the General College as well as his advisor. He wanted to convince Hovde to let him transfer next quarter to the university's College of Agriculture, to major in forestry. After a long discussion, Dr. Hovde thought he could see a pearl in the oyster. Recognizing that Norm was in earnest about what he wanted to achieve, Hovde gave his agreement.

Norman Borlaug now had an objective, a future.

Many years later, in1968, Borlaug visited the campus of Purdue University, where Dr. Hovde was president, to give the keynote address at the national convention of the American Phytopathology Society. While on campus he said to Vice President for Research Frederick Andrews, who was his guide, "While I'm here I'd like to see President Hovde."

"Well, excellent," agreed Andrews. "Do you know President Hovde?"

"Oh, yes," Borlaug replied. "He was my counselor when I was a freshman in the General College at the University of Minnesota. And I wouldn't be a scientist today if it weren't for Fred Hovde."[3]

Two years later, Dr. Hovde must have beamed with pride when Borlaug was awarded the Nobel Peace Prize.

Borlaug joined the wrestling team at the University of Minnesota. He says, "There were no athletic scholarships at the time; it was all amateur." He soon gained recognition in the sport, thanks to the excellent training he had received from Bartelma at Cresco High. He won his first intercollegiate match. To celebrate, he asked Margaret to a movie. She recalls that they held hands in the theater that night.

Borlaug became a star on the university's wrestling team, going so far as the Big Ten semifinals. His superior record won him a place in the Minnesota Athletic Hall of Fame, the Iowa Wrestling Hall of Fame, and the National Wrestling Hall of Fame in Stillwater, Oklahoma. As a sophomore, his outstanding record was influential in bringing Bartelma to the University of Minnesota as head wrestling coach. Together, Bartelma and Borlaug established and organized high school wrestling in the state of Minnesota.

During the school year 1935, Norman and Margaret saw each other regularly. They occasionally met on campus, and they spent an hour or two together on most Sundays. She took pride in his victories in wrestling and was nearly always among the spectators in support of her favorite. During that year the couple came to an understanding—they would get married when the time was right. Norm was determined to secure a future before he would ask her to marry him. Margaret says, "That seemed quite sensible to me. I was willing to wait."

Norman as the University of Minnesota's wrestling champ.

In December, Margaret decided not to continue her university studies. She said to Norm, "It means too much scrimping and saving. I cannot tolerate it any longer." With the help of her brother Bill, who was sports announcer at the University of Minnesota radio station and editor of the university's alumni magazine, she was able to get a job as a junior proofreader for a book press. She enjoyed reading and though the pay was low it would cover the living expenses in her one-room apartment.

To help with tuition, Norm applied for and received meager financial assistance from a National Youth Administration (NYA) program for college students with good academic records that Eleanor Roosevelt had successfully battled through Congress. The program paid fifteen cents an hour for part-time jobs, not as cash, but as credit toward tuition. Every little bit helped.

Norm says, "NYA is what saved me. And it was a valuable education within itself. We worked for different professors. I worked for a while with a veterinarian, another time with an entomologist. Those experiences helped round out my education."

During the summer and fall of 1936, to earn some money, Norm took a job at the Northeastern Forest Experiment Station at Williamstown, Massachusetts. He mapped and took the forest inventory on twenty farms that were to become the Hopkins Memorial Forest.

Then, during the summer of 1937, he got a job with the US Forest Service as a "look-out" at a link in the fire-protection network of the Idaho National Forest, on Cold Mountain in the Salmon River district of Idaho, at "the most isolated post in the USA." After training, he traveled forty-five miles by saddle horse from the Big Creek Ranger Station. A pack-horse driver accompanied him for the two-day journey over trackless country to his cabin on Cold Mountain. As the packman prepared to depart, following a night's sleep in the cabin, he said, "See ya in about six weeks when I bring supplies."

Borlaug was alone. He would spend the summer watching for lightning-set fires, fighting fires, studying the flora and fauna, and maintaining telephone and radio communication about his observations. In reflecting on the experience later, he said, "I lived and worked as a forester in the largest, most remote and undisturbed primitive or wilderness area in the lower forty-eight states of the USA, and it was there where I learned firsthand about oversimplification of the cliché, 'in balance with nature.' To this day I enjoy nature, the luxury of undisturbed wilderness, forests, mountains, lakes, rivers and deserts and their wildlife. But I also know that the greatest danger to their perpetuity is the pressure of human population."

His performance during the summer of 1937 won him a job offer. Starting in January 1938 he would be a full-time assistant ranger in the Idaho National Forest after completing his bachelor's degree at the end of 1937. Norm jumped at the chance.

As soon as he got back to Minneapolis, he told Margaret about the offer of steady work. Then he said, with gusto, "There's no reason for us to wait any more. Will you marry me?"

Margaret scheduled the event for the following Friday evening, September 27. Her brother Bill offered his sitting room for the service. Norm's two sisters, Palma and Charlotte, came up by train. A local Lutheran minister presided as the bride and groom gave their vows and then kissed each other tenderly. After a brief

Mr. and Mrs. Norman E. Borlaug.

reception they retired to Margaret's one-room apartment—their first home during their married life—for a weekend "honeymoon." There was neither time nor money for a romantic trip. That would have to wait. "But," Norm says, "we did attend the University of Minnesota football game and the Gophers won!"

Margaret's apartment, complete with a bathroom down the hall, shared by another family, was quite adequate as a temporary abode. They would soon be going west to enjoy the luxury of pristine wilderness.

By coincidence during the fall quarter of 1937, Borlaug met someone who was to have a profound impact on his life: Dr. E.C. Stakman, head of the department of plant pathology and one of the most respected scientists in the field. Early in the twentieth century, Dr. Stakman had established vital facts about wheat rust disease. As a high-school teacher on summer and Christmas vacations—with no funding—he surveyed rust-ravaged wheat from Minnesota south to Texas and on to the West Coast. He traveled six hundred miles by horse and buggy and slept in farmers' haystacks. Afterward, he joined the faculty of the University of Minnesota in 1909 and received its first Ph.D. in plant pathology in 1913. Until shortly before he died in 1979 at age 93, he kept regular office hours in what is now Stakman Hall.[4]

Stakman had seen Norm in a university wrestling match. He was impressed by his courage and tenacity. When he saw Borlaug in a forest pathology laboratory, he asked him a series of questions about the morphology of white pine wood samples, including questions designed to see what Norman might know about rusts—the parasitic fungal diseases of trees. Norm wondered how a plant pathologist would know so much about wood anatomy and structure.

Several weeks later Norm learned that Professor Stakman

was to give the Sigma Xi Lecture: "The Shifty Little Enemies [rusts] that Destroy our Cereal Crops." In pioneering research on rust diseases in crops, "Stak" and his collaborators had developed an understanding of the epidemiology of stem rust in the great plains of the USA and Canada. They had discovered that races existed within the rust organism, which explained how new races could attack previously rust-resistant crop varieties; and that new races were formed through hybridization on barberry bushes—the alternate host of the disease.

Stakman was a compelling lecturer and teacher as well as a brilliant scientist. Norm was thrilled to be in his audience.

During his lecture Stakman said, "Rust is a shifty, changing, constantly evolving enemy; we can never lower our guard. We must fight rust by all means open to science."

As Norm enthusiastically related parts of Stakman's lecture to Margaret, he declared: "One day I would like to go back and study under that man if it is ever possible."

During his last days at college, Norman was confident of getting his degree. He would soon be off to his new job. Then, about a week before Christmas, Norm received a devastating shock. A letter from the supervisor of the Idaho National Forest said that due to budget cuts the junior forester position could not be funded. There would be no position for him until June.

What was he to do now?

Margaret pleaded with him to begin immediately doing postgraduate work at the university. They could keep on living in the one-room apartment. She would hold on to her job as a proofreader. She said, "I'll go on working for a while. I enjoy it; you know that. Sitting there all day reading all kinds of interesting things." She said her wages would be enough for them both.

"Go and do six months of postgraduate work, Norman.

That will give you an objective."

Norm's confidence was restored by Margaret's persuasive encouragement. Next morning he knocked on Dr. Stakman's door. "Professor Stakman, I've been thinking I would like to stay on and work on a master's degree. After my experience the last two summers in the Forest Service, seeing the destruction of chestnut and American elm trees by disease in the Eastern USA, and white pine diseases in Idaho, I would like to study forest pathology. What do you think?"

"I tell you what I think. I think most forest pathologists starve to death. You should go into plant pathology—that will give you more flexibility."

Stakman encouraged Borlaug to enroll in a master's program. The professor would find him a paid assistantship for the coming year.

Borlaug was delighted. He enrolled for the year and before long Stakman found him a research assistantship in the department of plant pathology. In addition to a small salary, his tuition was waived.

Princess Serendip had smiled on the Iowa farm boy.

Norm received his master's degree in 1940. He was designated an instructor and was assigned a two-room university-owned apartment while he pursued a doctorate in general plant pathology.

In October 1941, while still writing his doctoral dissertation, Norm was invited for an interview in Wilmington, Delaware with E. I. DuPont de Nemours & Company. Following the interview he was offered $2,800 per year as head of a biochemical laboratory to start an active program in agricultural chemicals. The sum sounded enormous to Norm. After he and Margaret discussed the offer, Norm readily accepted. He would finish his dissertation in a month or two and receive his Ph.D. the following year.

The young couple packed their few belongings in a newly acquired 1935 Pontiac and headed for Wilmington. With a secure future, they could now start a family.

Chapter Three

The Rockefeller Foundation Offers Borlaug a Challenge

"My work to combat hunger started in Mexico with the Rockefeller Foundation. Inspired by Henry Wallace, it was the first ever attempt to help food deficit nations by a foreign organization."

—Norman Borlaug

Norman Borlaug settled in quickly with his new responsibilities at DuPont. He enjoyed serving as quarterback in his laboratory, delegating and monitoring tasks. He soon finished writing his dissertation and sent it to Professor Stakman. Norm's graduate committee approved the study and recommended that he be awarded a degree. "Norm-boy" became Dr. Norman Ernest Borlaug. Norm says, "Sadly, Granddad Nels had left us in 1935, so he could not share the laurels."

A few months later, Margaret announced to the new Dr. Borlaug that he was going to be a father. To her parents' delight, Norma Jean Borlaug was born on September 27, 1943.

Norm had been productively employed in defense work at DuPont for a little more than two years when, out of the blue, he was faced with an immense challenge. People in Mexico were hungry. George Harrar, a protégé and former graduate student of E.C. Stakman's at the University of Minnesota, had been hired by the Rockefeller Foundation[5] to organize a team of scientists to lead a conquest against the endemic hunger south of the border. With Professor Stakman at his side, Harrar set out to try to hire Borlaug as the team's plant pathologist.

As they sat quietly at dinner that evening, Norm shared with Margaret the day's discussion that he had had with Harrar and Stakman. He said, "It sounds interesting, but I told them I cannot leave this position at DuPont because it is under the War Manpower Control Program."

The world was at war. And much of the world was on the verge of starvation. Mexico, in America's backyard, was critically short on food. India and China were losing the battle in their attempts to match food production with population growth. Russia had buried thousands upon thousands of peasants who had succumbed to starvation. The USA was shipping food to war-torn Europe.

President Franklin D. Roosevelt's vice president-elect and former Secretary of Agriculture, Henry A. Wallace, had a vision. He had an uncanny ability to see beyond the hunger problems—to foresee a future made brighter by focused agricultural research. In brief, his ideas centered on technologies for producing more and better food. He envisioned a program to guarantee adequate food supplies for all the peoples of the world.[6]

Henry Wallace's vision served as a catalyst that sparked the Rockefeller Foundation to field a team of agricultural scientists, including Norman Borlaug, to Mexico to take up the challenge of relieving hunger in that neighboring country. Wallace would not live to see it, but the efforts of that team a quarter century later would lead to the dramatic reversal from widespread starvation to self-sufficiency in basic foodstuffs in India, Pakistan and a number of other countries as well as in Mexico. Following is the chain of events that put Norman Borlaug on a path that allowed his multifaceted talents to blossom and for which he was ultimately awarded the Nobel Peace Prize.

Henry Wallace had studied agriculture at Iowa State College. After graduating in 1910, he started experimenting with hybrid corn. In 1923, he developed the first commercially viable strain of hybrid corn. In 1926, he founded the Hi Bred Corn Company, now Pioneer Hi-Bred International. He started a revolution in corn production, first in Iowa and then throughout the Midwest.

In 1933, less than 1 percent of corn planted in the US Corn Belt was hybrid. Within ten years the percentage rose to 78. In Iowa, which led the way, it was 99.5 percent. Henry Wallace did not invent hybrid corn, but more than any other one person he was responsible for developing the technology of hybrid corn seed and expanding its use.[7] In 1931, the average corn yield in the United States was twenty-four bushels per acre, about the same as at the conclusion of the Civil War. A decade later corn yield had increased to thirty-one bushels per acre. Due to a large extent to the transition from open pollinated varieties to hybrids—and with the use of mineral fertilizer—the average yield had grown to one hundred ten bushels by 1981.

Following his election as vice president in early November 1940 and prior to his being sworn in, Henry Wallace was unemployed. To improve his fluency in Spanish, he decided to take a trip to Latin America, perhaps Costa Rica or Guatemala. When he announced this to Roosevelt, the president suggested he go to Mexico instead, where he could serve as "Ambassador Extraordinary" for the December 1st inauguration of General Manuel Avila Camacho as president of Mexico.[8] Wallace agreed.

Wallace and his wife, Ilo, drove their own car to Mexico City, without any security, so that Henry could stop en route to chat, in Spanish, with Mexican children and farmers and observe their agriculture, especially the cornfields. He became intrigued with what he saw. After the inauguration, the Wallaces stayed for a few weeks as guests of the US ambassador. During that time, Wallace conducted a personal inspection tour of Mexican agriculture. He walked up steep hillsides to see the corn grown in mountainous areas. He talked with local farmers and visited the leading agricultural college at Chapingo. He studied the Mexican diet and observed farm implements and work patterns. He also met with and discussed agriculture and food problems with outgoing President Lazaro Cardenes and Secretary of Agriculture Inginero Marte R. Gomez, who had been the two most important officials in implementing the agrarian reform to redistribute land following the revolution. They were concerned because per capita food production was falling despite the agrarian reforms.

In the native land of corn domestication, Wallace came away appalled. The very best farms he saw produced only twenty bushels to the acre. Most Mexican farms produced only ten bushels per acre.

At the time, 80 percent of Mexicans lived on the land and the poorer people depended for their subsistence largely on corn and beans. Wallace became absorbed with the critical problem of poor nutrition in Mexico. He exchanged thoughts on the subject with members of a Rockefeller Foundation team that had been in Mexico for about two decades as part of a cooperative public health program.

Wallace returned to Washington in early January. Before he was sworn in as vice president he began to do something about the conditions he had seen in Mexico. He recognized that with war clouds on the horizon, he would not be able to get a bill through Congress to sponsor and finance assistance for our southern neighbor to solve its agriculture and food problems. He asked the Rockefeller Foundation if they might help.

On February 3, 1941, Raymond B. Fosdick, president of the Rockefeller Foundation, met in Washington with Vice President Wallace to explore how the Foundation might be able to improve nutrition in Mexico. Wallace said raising the yields of maize (corn), wheat and beans would have a more positive effect on the lives of Mexico's poor than anything else that could be done. He suggested that the Foundation shift from emphasis on health in Mexico to assistance with food production. Otherwise, they would end up "with population crowding on the means of subsistence."

Meanwhile, Mexico's Minister of Agriculture Marte R. Gomez asked the Rockefeller Foundation for help with their perplexing nutrition issues; he especially requested help to increase corn yields, since that basic food grain was in seriously short supply.

The Rockefeller Foundation quickly took up the challenge. Ray Fosdick called a staff meeting at Rockefeller Foundation headquarters in New York. In keeping with the foundation's "basic policy of knowing the facts before going into action… [and that] promising men and creative ideas are basic and fundamental," they decided to send a strong team on a survey mission to Mexico. The team's mission would be to study the agriculture and food situation and make recommendations.[9]

The Foundation hired the University of Minnesota's Professor E. C. Stakman, who by this time was internationally recognized for his pioneering work in plant pathology, and who spoke six languages including Spanish, to form and lead a team to analyze the situation in Mexico. Besides Stakman and some Mexican scientists, the group included Richard Bradfield, Professor of Soil Science at Cornell, and Paul C. Mangelsdorf, Professor of Plant Genetics and Economic Botany at Harvard.[10] Like Stakman, both Bradfield and Mangelsdorf had international reputations, had traveled widely, and had an interest in the developing nations of the world.

Dr. Stakman's team met with officials of the government of Mexico to discuss possible joint collaboration. During several months in 1941 the team, together with Mexican scientists, studied the situation in sixteen of Mexico's thirty-three states. Then Stakman recommended a plan of action: the Foundation should field an in-country team of four dedicated and competent scientists. They would cooperate with Mexico's Ministry of Agriculture in developing improved plant varieties, especially for the principal food crops, corn and wheat, with some attention to beans and a few other crops. They would also explore issues of soil improvement and crop management.

The proposed program for the Foundation was indeed a new venture. The only previous Rockefeller Foundation program in international agriculture was in China in 1935. It was a distributive program, limited to providing funds. In Mexico, the Foundation agreed to provide assistance to direct and operate the program as well as to provide funds.

Discussions in 1943 resulted in the Mexican Government-Rockefeller Foundation Cooperative Agricultural Program. This would be America's first foreign agricultural assistance program.[11]

Recognizing that quality of staff is the critical factor in determining the ultimate success of a program, the Rockefeller Foundation then asked Dr. Stakman to identify the best man possible to lead the project. He recommended J. George "Dutch" Harrar, who in 1935 had earned a Ph.D. as one of Stakman's students at the University of Minnesota. Harrar was young, physically strong and intellectually tough. After getting his master's degree at Iowa State and before going to the University of Minnesota, Harrar spent four years in Puerto Rico teaching and working on plant diseases and botany. He spoke fluent Spanish. After earning his Ph.D., Harrar had been a professor for five years at Virginia Polytechnic Institute. At age thirty-six he had just been appointed head of the Department of Plant Pathology at Washington State University. He was embarked on a promising career.

After thinking it over, Harrar accepted Stakman's challenge. In February 1943, he and Stakman set out on a three-month survey of Mexico to lay the basic groundwork for their program. They presented a plan of operation to the Mexican government. It called for creating a new organization—Office of Special Studies—to operate within Mexico's Ministry of Agriculture, but to be run by Harrar under the direction of the Rockefeller Foundation in cooperation with the government of Mexico. The scientific focus would be on increasing corn, bean and wheat production, soil fertility and agronomy, and plant pathology. The Office was to be staffed jointly by Mexicans and Americans. Emphasis would be on training young Mexicans who, it was planned, would eventually take over the project.

In a brief biography of Harrar, John McKelvey says it was "strange that the Foundation should have chosen George to head a practical program in agriculture. He was city bred; he had no farm experience; he had graduated from a liberal arts college [Oberlin]; and in his research in graduate school and his subsequent assignments at the University of Puerto Rico and VPI, he had focused—and published—mainly on mycological problems associated with plant diseases rather than on pragmatic problems of producing basic food crops."

McKelvey continues. "The choice was not so strange, however, when one considers three things: George's total dedication to a task at hand; his growing awareness through his land-grant college assignments of the vital importance of a healthy agriculture to the welfare of a country; and his reputation as a proven scientist."[12]

Harrar led the pioneering program from 1943 to 1952, when the Foundation asked him to go to its home office in New York as the Deputy Director for Agriculture. In New York, Harrar went up the line to become the Foundation's president, a post he served from 1961 until 1972.

Harrar reflected later on the beginning of his assignment in Mexico: "My first associate was a young Mexican graduate of the National School of Agriculture... Later we were joined by additional expatriate staff specialists in corn, wheat, soil science, entomology, and plant pathology. Each of these specialists became the leader of a small group of young Mexican agronomists assigned by the Ministry for training."[13]

During the next several years, the number of young Mexican colleagues on the team grew to more than two hundred, and some fifty Latin Americans came from other countries to work and study with the group in Mexico.

In mid-1943, Harrar went to the States to seek more scientists for his team in three major areas of concern: soil fertility, corn production, and disease control, especially on wheat. Stakman and Mangelsdorf recommended he try for Dr. Edwin J. Wellhausen, a geneticist-corn breeder, and Dr. William Colwell, an agronomist-soil scientist. Both Wellhausen and Colwell, each of whom had farm backgrounds, accepted the assignment.

For the plant pathologist, Stakman recommended Dr. Norman E. Borlaug. He told Harrar that Borlaug had been a keen student who had shown a special interest in plant diseases, including wheat rust, which Stakman had observed to be a major problem in Mexico. He said, "He will not be defeated by difficulty and he burns with a missionary zeal."

Today, Borlaug says he still recalls one of Stakman's lectures in 1938 in which he characterized the disease, wheat rust, as "a shifty, changing, constantly evolving enemy." Little did Norman know that he would spend much of the rest of his life battling this "enemy" of food production worldwide.

Rusts afflict most major crop plants. They are caused by fungi that need living host tissue for their growth, development and reproduction. Wheat is damaged by three species: stem rust, leaf rust, and stripe rust. Rusts get their name from the dry, dusty red-to-yellow appearance of stripes or spots that erupt through the tissues of the wheat plant. Rusts diminish plant vigor and limit the maturation of grain formation and filling. Plant growth and productivity are seriously inhibited or killed by this destructive disease.

Harrar, with Stakman at his side, set out to try to hire Borlaug away from his position at DuPont. Harrar told Borlaug the team he was putting together was "going to conquer hunger in Mexico; those people need help badly; the opportunities for worthwhile work are enormous. I would like for you to work on diseases of all crops in our program, with special emphasis on wheat."

When Borlaug asked for Stakman's advice, the professor said, "Norman, you are the best man for the job. You have excellent background and training in plant breeding and pathology; you have broad interests in land use from agriculture to forestry, and you have the energy and motivation. It's a tough, demanding task you're being offered. It's a long, grinding project. But if I can encourage you, Norman, I'll say this: it would be a worthwhile thing to do, to put bread into those hungry bellies in Mexico."

At dinner that evening, Norm shared with Margaret the day's discussion with Harrar and Stakman. Then he said, "Why should I give up a good job with DuPont just to 'put bread into those hungry bellies in Mexico'? Hell, I've never even been to Mexico and I don't know a word of Spanish."

Margaret countered, "But Norman, you know you've always felt a need to do something to help hungry people." She also knew that Norman was disappointed when DuPont had to switch his laboratory from working on agricultural chemicals to defense work after Pearl Harbor.

"But what about you and Jeanie," Norm said, "and what about the baby we're expecting in a couple of months? How would you handle that in a strange country?"

Margaret was calm, self-assured and devoted to her husband. She knew Norm would like to give this new challenge a try, and she encouraged him. She understood that her husband was concerned for her and the baby, but she recognized the inevitability of his need to take on new challenges. She said, "You don't need to worry about me, Norman. You know full well I'm quite capable of taking care of myself. Now you go. I'll join you when you get settled."

With Margaret's robust encouragement, Norm accepted Harrar's offer when he was released from War Manpower Control on July 1st.

In September 1944, leaving behind his pregnant wife and one-year-old Jeanie, Borlaug drove to the Mexican border at Laredo, Texas, where Ed Wellhausen and his wife Vivian were waiting for him. At dinner that evening Ed described the difficulties of working in Mexico. Even though their "Office" was semi-autonomous, dealing with the Mexican bureaucracy "is a pain in the neck; it's like punching a featherbed."

Norm called Margaret from his hotel room in Mexico City to enquire how she and Jeanie were getting along. "We're doing fine, Norman," she said. "How about yourself? What's it like down there?"

Norm summarized for her what he had learned from Ed during the three-day drive from the Texas border to Mexico City: "It looks like it's going to be an uphill struggle to get this project off the ground. There are no modern experimental field stations and there are only a few trained Mexican agronomists. The 800 acres of land surrounding the agricultural school at Chapingo, twenty miles northeast of Mexico City, is mostly unused and choked with weeds. Harrar has been given 150 acres there to set up an experimental corn and wheat breeding station, but there's not any equipment. The Rockefeller Foundation can't help with tractors, trucks or major farm equipment because the US government has these on wartime priority. Gasoline and spare tires are nearly impossible to obtain. The only building is an adobe shed with a tar-paper roof that has just been built by Harrar and Wellhausen.

"Ed says the minister of agriculture, Dr. Marte R. Gomez, is eager to cooperate, but the bureaucracy moves slowly. All in all, it's not a very encouraging situation. Ed says we'll just have to do what we can with what we have."

After saying goodnight to Margaret and Jeanie, Norm reflected further on Wellhausen's briefing. He didn't sleep well that night.

The project's first exerimental station.

The next day Wellhausen drove Norm to San Jacinto, a suburb of Mexico City, to the Office of Special Studies. George Harrar welcomed Norm with a strong handshake and broad grin and introduced him to William Colwell, the soil scientist. Harrar said, "Our first problem is to inject a little modernity into this out-of-date agricultural system."

Harrar spent much of the day giving Norm background on Mexico's bloody revolution of 1910-1918, which ended with a land distribution program that transferred some fifty million hectares from the large landowners and from church lands to a new class of small-scale farmers—the *campesinos*. He explained that most of these former feudal peons lacked the knowledge, skills and money needed to make their small patches viable. After thirty years, the reforms in which so much hope had been vested had failed to end poverty, ignorance and hunger.

"In this atmosphere," Harrar said, "we've committed ourselves to fomenting the country's first bloodless revolution—offering the possibility of doubling food production through a transformation of technology."

As he went to bed in the Hotel Geneve, which would be his home for the next three months, Norm thought, "What kind of future is there for me in this strange country?"

During his first weeks in Mexico, Borlaug worked with Wellhausen in the experimental station at Chapingo, developing a network of roads and underground irrigation systems, and preparing for the first experimental wheat plantings in November. He and Harrar concentrated on wheat, Wellhausen on corn and Colwell on soil-fertility tests.

In an attempt to broaden their base of operations, Borlaug and Wellhausen went into the great central agricultural region, the Bajio, to try to enlist farmers to allow them to plant test plots of corn and wheat on their land. They would evaluate the responses of different varieties to various altitudes and soil conditions, and in the process would demonstrate improved crop production technologies to local farmers.

What they found was shocking. Hopelessness pervaded the lives of most of the people. The land was mostly devoid of nutrients; fertilizer was largely unknown and in any case was too expensive. The people needed food. Four out of five could not read or write.

There was no international telephone service outside Mexico City, so before he went to bed that night, Norm wrote to Margaret: "These places I've seen have clubbed my mind—they are so poor and depressing. No wonder the people are the way they are! Can you imagine a poor Mexican guy struggling to feed his family? I don't know what we can do to help these people, but we've got to do something."

Norm didn't mention to Margaret that he was ill—weakened by the ravages of dysentery and constant nausea. He didn't want her to worry. Somehow he forgot his own discomfort as he saw the human misery around him.

Then, on November 9, Norm had a distressing phone call from Margaret. What had been expected to be a blessing turned out to be a trauma; baby Scott had arrived and was diagnosed with a rare and fatal disease, spina bifida, an incomplete closure of the spinal column. Of the three types of the malady, Scott's was the most severe. There was no cure. In tears, Margaret said, "Norman, the doctor says there is no hope for Scotty; it's a matter of a few weeks—a few months at most."

Norm was devastated. Margaret assured him that she could handle the situation. She would postpone joining him in Mexico until things sorted out. She wanted to be sure that the baby had proper care.

Norm borrowed some money and flew back to Wilmington to spend a week with Margaret, Jeanie and little Scotty.

After a few weeks, Margaret's doctor urged her to go join Norman. He said, "There is nothing medically that can be done for Scotty; it's just a matter of time. It would be best if you left him here in the hospital and joined your husband." The doctor assured Margaret that the baby would receive good care and, when he passed on, as he would soon, he would be given a proper burial.

Margaret was torn between staying with Scott and going to be with Norman. She soon decided it was best to take the doctor's advice. She and Jeanie went by train to Mexico City. Norman met and embraced them and took them to their new apartment. Several months later, Dr. Wagner sent word that little Scott had died peacefully; the body was buried as Margaret had specified.

Life for the Borlaugs once again approached normality.

In March 1945, George Harrar said to Borlaug, "I've got too much to handle at the Office of Special Studies. I want you to take over the wheat program."

Norm had his work cut out for him.

Chapter Four

Borlaug Builds a Revolutionary Wheat-Breeding Program

"Goddammit, Norm, this scheme of yours has been considered twice, at your insistence, and voted down twice. Why can't you accept that?"

—J. George Harrar

Within a decade after arriving in Mexico as a thirty-year-old scientist, Norman Borlaug had embarked on three innovations that formed the foundation of a wheat revolution in Mexico and ultimately fostered the Green Revolution in Asia. First, he painstakingly crossed thousands upon thousands of varieties and moved forward with a few that were rust-resistant. Next, he started a "shuttle breeding" program that cut in half the time needed to get results and, fortuitously, resulted in the seeds being rust-resistant and globally adaptable. Then, he changed the architecture of the wheat plant from gangly tall to a short-strawed, heavy tillering structure that was suitable for machine harvesting and was responsive to heavy applications of fertilizer without falling over. Yields skyrocketed.

In reflecting on the experience, Borlaug says, "In 1944, I resigned from a challenging research position in the agricultural chemical division of E. I. DuPont de Nemours & Co. to accept a position with the Rockefeller Foundation as plant pathologist with the Cooperative Mexican-Rockefeller Foundation Agricultural Program. I accepted the job sight unseen, without ever having visited Mexico, without speaking a word of Spanish.

"Many times during the next four years, frustrated by unavailability of machinery and equipment, without the assistance of trained scientists, traveling over bad roads, living in miserable hotels, eating bad food, often sick with diarrhea and unable to communicate because of lack of command of the language, I was certain I had made a dreadful mistake in resigning from my former position. However, by 1948, research results, the bits and pieces of the wheat production puzzle, began to emerge, and the fog of gloom and despair began to lift. I began to see rays of sunlight and hope."

In the spring of 1945, after Borlaug had been in Mexico about six months, George Harrar assigned him the task of organizing and directing the Cooperative Wheat Research and Production Program.[14] With Harrar as supervisor, the Rockefeller Foundation's mandate to Borlaug was to do whatever was necessary to increase Mexico's wheat production. He would work across a broad spectrum of disciplines: scientific research in genetics, plant breeding, plant pathology, entomology, agronomy, soil science, and cereal technology.

In practice, Norm did all the above plus whatever else was needed to get wheat production up—experimental plot development, planting, recruiting helpers, and training young scientists and technicians. He and his team began planting demonstration plots on farmers' fields, employing a package of improved technology: seed of better varieties, fertilizer, improved irrigation practices, and weed control.

Borlaug worked from the ground up. From the very first

days of his assignment in Mexico, he gave his young Mexican colleagues in the Office of Special Studies the opportunity and responsibility to learn, to become proficient in the secrets of plant breeding—crossing and selection—the critical steps that most plant breeders kept to themselves. He says, "Alongside our own work we were to train local scientists and ease them into our jobs. Moreover, we were to be neither consultants nor advisors, but working scientists getting our hands and boots dirty, and demonstrating by our own field results what could be done."

Norm met some resistance to this approach. In the Mexican culture, scientists were above hand labor or getting dirty. In Latin cultures, a manager was designated as a "limpio saco," or clean shirt, to distinguish him from his inferiors. One of Norm's Mexican colleagues said to him in the early days of the program, "Dr. Borlaug, we don't do these things in Mexico. That's why we have peons. All you've got to do is draw up the plans and take them to the foreman and let them do it."

The normally calm Dr. Borlaug lost his temper and raised his voice. "That's why the farmers have no respect for you. If you don't know how to do something properly yourself, how can you possibly advise them? If the peons give you false information, you wouldn't even know. No, this has to change. Until we master our own efforts, we will go nowhere in this project."

Norm got his point across. From that day on, the Mexican scientists worked in the field side by side with Borlaug.

First Innovation: High-volume Crossbreeding

A serious problem in Mexico that caused enormous fluctuations in yields was epidemics of wheat rust, Professor Stakman's shifty enemy. Stem rust often blasted the wheat plants before harvest and turned the fields to sickly gray instead of a field of golden grain. Tragically, stem rust generally was deadliest in exactly those areas where wheat was potentially most productive. Two other kinds of rust—brown leaf rust and yellow stripe rust—were seldom as devastating as stem rust.[15]

The native wheats were susceptible to many races of the stem-rust organism. In three years, from 1939 to 1942, stem rust had slashed Mexico's national wheat harvest in half. Losses were greatest in Sonora, the most important wheat production region. Much of the former wheat land had been given over to flax, cotton, and other crops, which fared only somewhat better.

The objective of Borlaug's first innovation, then, was to breed varieties of wheat that were resistant to stem rust. His approach was to crossbreed hundreds and hundreds of different lines in hopes of finding a few, or even *one* that was resistant to prevalent rust races and yielded well.

Most plant breeders made only a few crosses or a few dozen crosses each season. Each of the many individual plants that resulted had to be observed throughout the growing season and seeds from the "best" individuals harvested and planted the next year, when more selections were made, a process that was then repeated for six to seven years. Norm couldn't wait that long. He had to speed the process. He collected thousands of varieties from widely varying wheat-producing areas throughout the world. He and his Mexican apostles began crossing them.

Borlaug says, "Crossbreeding is a hit-or-miss process. It's time consuming and mind-warpingly tedious. There's only one chance in thousands of ever finding what you want, and actually no guarantee of success at all."

Crossbreeding by hand is a delicate operation, performed with surgical-type tweezers. The breeder must remove the male stamen, which contains the immature pollen, from each bisexual wheat flower. Otherwise, the plant will pollinate itself. The emasculated wheat head is then covered with a small glassine bag to prevent promiscuous out-crossing with wind-blown pollen. After two days the pistil (ovary) of the emasculated flower is pollinated (fertilized) with pollen of the other parental variety.

Norm was willing to take on the immense amount of work this entailed. From daylight 'til sundown, he was bent over in the experimental wheat trials, making notes and recording differences in the varieties in resistance to rust disease. At the time of crossbreeding, he sometimes slept out at the field station in his sleeping bag and cooked his food over an open campfire, in effect reverting to his days as a forester. He went back to his hotel in Mexico City for a bath and hot meal only occasionally, when he could hitch a ride in the one-vehicle fleet that the Office of Special Studies had at that time.

Borlaug crossbreeding wheat.

The tedious work started to pay off. It resulted in the production of rust-resistant lines adapted to conditions in Mexico. Yields from the improved varieties ranged from 20 percent to more than 40 percent higher than the yields of those they replaced. Borlaug never wasted time searching for the perfect variety, but after adequate testing released for commercial use the best available at that point in time.

By 1952, Norm's log had entries for six thousand individual crosses of wheat heads. In carrying out this massive breeding program, Norm says he learned "to tell the status of a wheat plant from its look, manner of growth, disease reactions, feel, and movement. Wheat itself was becoming a person. Moreover, wheat was the best teacher about wheat." In his obsessive quest for viable stock, Norm began to perceive that different wheats had different "personalities." He could tell them apart at a glance, by knowing who some of their parents or grandparents were, or even by the rustle of the wind through their ripening heads.

One day, several Chapingo college staff members visited the experimental grounds. Summing up the efforts he had made so far, Norm told them, "There are millions of wheat plants here. Each head will grow a couple of dozen grains of seed—and there will not be one seed in billions that will be totally acceptable for what we need in Mexico. Perfection is a butterfly the academics chase and never catch. If we go on looking for the ideal wheat for Mexico, your countrymen will go on being hungry for a long time. We will have to do the best we can with what we have."[16]

A few days later, one of those who had heard Norm's talk at the experimental station, Pablo Maurer, who had been a student at Texas A&M University, brought his brother, Roberto Maurer, to see Norm. Roberto had a one-hundred-hectare tract in the Yaqui Valley, near the town of Ciudad Obregon, in the state of Sonora in northwestern Mexico. For the past few years, he had grown a number of varieties of wheat, but the pernicious rust, other diseases and other problems resulted in low yields. Only one variety had shown any signs of resistance, and it had many defects.

Borlaug had heard that Don Rodolfo Elias Calles, son of Mexico's President Calles, had established a showcase experimental station near the city of Ciudad Obregon in the Yaqui Valley in 1934 while he was Governor of Sonora. He decided to go see it.

Norm also wanted to find out more about Roberto Maurer's experience with wheat. But it was not easy to get to Obregon from Mexico City. The journey of two thousand kilometers on rugged cross-country roads was impractical. He learned that a tri-motor Fokker, a lumbering, privately owned plane, ran a shuttle service twice a week from Mexico City to Ciudad Obregon. It could get him to his destination in two days. He packed his bedroll and some canned food and took the plane. It landed near the city of Ciudad Obregon on a narrow dirt strip cut between wheat fields, about twenty-five kilometers from the government experiment station.

The Yaqui Valley land had good soil, and irrigation water was available in much of the area. It looked like promising wheat land, but only if high-yielding, stem-rust-resistant varieties could be made available. There had been three disastrous stem-rust epidemics between 1939 and 1942.

Borlaug hitched a ride to the experimental station that Governor Calles had built in the mid-1930s to help farmers in the area. When he saw it, his heart sank. The once beautiful research station that was a model for all Latin America when it was developed became a shambles of neglect, weeds interspersed among sorry-looking test plots, after the station's one scientist was transferred to Mexico City.

Norm's home for the next several days would be the abandoned, rat-infested headquarters of the research station. He heated a can of beans for supper and retired early in his bedroll.

Next morning he visited local farms, quizzed the operators, collected heads of wheat, labeled them and stashed them in his bag. After three days of visiting farms, he found Roberto Maurer working his wheat fields. Roberto, who had spent several years in school in Canada and spoke English, was surprised and delighted to see him and invited him to his house for a meal. Roberto's attractive young wife, Teresa, greeted Norm warmly. This was the beginning of a lifelong friendship with the couple.

From his trip to Sonora, Norm had in mind a concept—shuttle breeding—that might speed the process of developing new wheat varieties for Mexico. If it worked, it could cut in half the usual seven to eight years. But he was not yet ready to discuss these ideas with anyone. He wanted to develop the plan more thoroughly in his own mind and test its feasibility before showing it to his directors.

Second Innovation: Shuttle Breeding

Borlaug's second breeding innovation had the initial objective of speeding the process by growing two successive plantings per year—one during summer in the low-soil-fertility, rainfed areas at Chapingo and Toluca, in high altitudes not far from Mexico City, and another during the winter season almost two thousand kilometers to the north, in the irrigated area near sea level in the Yaqui Valley in Sonora, where growing conditions and soil fertility were much more favorable.

Ever since his trip to Sonora he had been mulling over an idea he wanted to put to the test. He had brought back some wheat from the farms in the Yaqui Valley, and now, in May of 1946, he wanted to prepare a plot to plant it. If it grew well in the highlands of Chapingo or Toluca during the summer, he would gather the seed in the fall, take it north again, and plant it in the Yaqui. (Because of the difference in altitude and temperature, the Toluca and Yaqui planting seasons were at different times of the year.) The following spring the next generation would be harvested in the Yaqui and would be put into the soil at Toluca, and so on back and forth. It would mean that he could grow two generations a year instead of one, cutting his breeding time by half.[17]

It had not been tried before: two generations each year

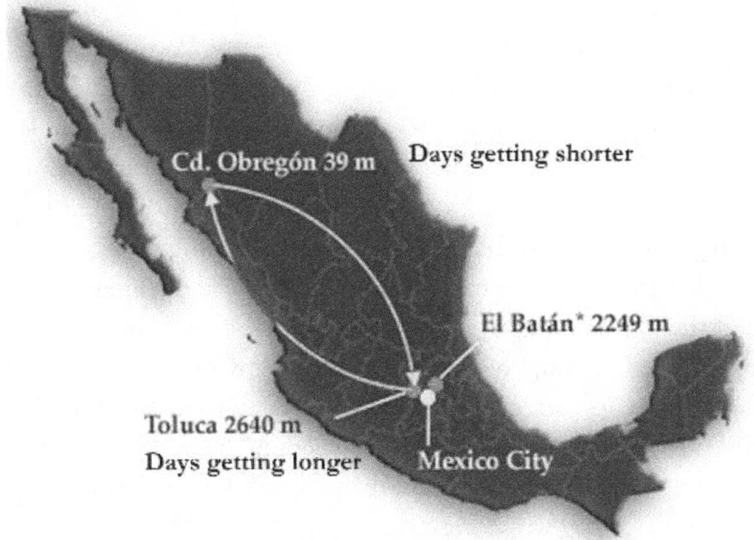

Shuttle breeding between Toluca and Obregon.

instead of one, plus a complete switch from one latitude and altitude to another. This concept flew in the face of traditional plant breeding methods, a dogma that precluded two generations per year. But Borlaug saw no genetic reason why he couldn't grow and select two generations each year. He would try it.

The Mexican foreman in charge of the work said, "But Borlaug, *señor*, no wheat is planted here in the summer. The rain and heat and the rust will kill it. You will waste time and work, *patron*."

Borlaug smiled and patted his friend's shoulder. "Tell you what, Manuel, *amigo*. You worry about getting that damn land in shape—and I'll worry about the rust. Okay?"

He went back to the shed and took out the seeds he had gathered from the fields of the Yaqui Valley. He sorted them out and planted them in ten different rows in the freshly turned earth. He labeled them according to variety and the fields from which they had come. When he finished, he looked up toward the heavens, crossed his fingers, and said to himself, *It's in your hands now, Lord.*

As the summer wore on, Borlaug kept a close eye on the small plots he had planted with seed from the Yaqui Valley. Contrary to the predictions of the foreman, Manuel, the wheat was thriving except for a few lines that were susceptible to and killed by rust. Here was living proof that he could grow two seasons of plants in a single year. Now he planned to take the next logical step and return it to the Yaqui Valley in the coming fall.

Borlaug had discussed his plan with Ed Wellhausen, who had the ear of the project director, Harrar, and was his closest confidant. Ed said, "Norm, the wind is blowing against your idea: doubling wheat-breeding seasons has more to it than planting; it will double the costs of fertilizer, weeding, harvesting and travel; and it will double the strain on the project's limited resources."

But Borlaug was determined.

He said, "Don't try to discourage me, Ed. I know how much work is involved. Don't tell me what can't be done. Tell me what needs to be done—and let me do it. There's one single factor that makes the Yaqui effort worth a try, and that's rust. Breeding two generations a year means beating and staying ahead of the shifty stem-rust organism. If I can lick that problem by working in Sonora, then we've won a victory. To hell with the extra work and strain. It's got to be done, and I believe I can do it."

Borlaug pressed ahead with the selection of seed for replanting in the Yaqui and made plans to fly north. He packed the seed from the first generation of Sonora wheats harvested at Toluca, and seed from the other strains bred in the Toluca station—the rust-resistant lines. Then in late October, he boarded the rickety tri-motor plane that took him once again to the airstrip near Ciudad Obregon. He planted two hectares of different breeding lines and varieties, then went back to work on the Toluca station and to be with Margaret and Jeanie.

George Harrar, the project director, had a tough job. He had to husband his resources—both men and materials. He worked hard and demanded the same hard work and self-sacrifice from his colleagues. In return, he allowed his staff plenty of freedom to work in whatever way suited them best. The exercise of this freedom ultimately brought Harrar and Borlaug into conflict.

Borlaug had imported a small thresher from Pullman, Washington, to harvest the wheat plantings during the summer at Chapingo. Now, he needed to move it to the Yaqui Valley for the winter harvest. Because of the difficulty of airfreighting the machine, he decided to go overland by truck for the first time. Arrangements would have to be made through Harrar at the Office of Special Studies. This led to the first open opposition to his plans for work in Sonora.

Harrar shook his head. "It's far too risky to go overland on the west coast road, it's too expensive, and living in the Yaqui Valley of Sonora would be too difficult for our families." Without pausing for Norm's reaction, he continued, "Listen, Norm, it makes no sense to risk a round trip of four thousand kilometers through that country. You could lose everything—and for what? The guts of our problem is here, in the poverty areas. We've got to win our fight right here, in the breadbasket of the Bajio region and the high valleys. You've got to get that clear."

There followed a clash of wills between two strong-minded men.

Norm said, "I'm going north because there's potential there. We cannot produce the wheat that Mexico needs without Sonora. What we do there will soon be followed in the Bajio. I'm going there because I think I can lick stem rust up there and increase production rapidly. And I'm going because I think it's right."

Fortunately, Dr. Stakman was visiting at the time.

Harrar shrugged and looked at Stakman. Then he said, "Well, okay, go ahead and try it, but I don't think it's a good idea."

The issue was not settled, just postponed.

During the summer of 1948, the three-man Rockefeller Foundation agricultural advisory committee—Stakman, Bradfield, and Mangelsdorf—met with the Office of Special Studies team in Mexico City. The committee was joined by Dr. H. K. Hayes, a plant geneticist from the University of Minnesota. Hayes held strong views against the "shuttle breeding" plan, and Norm knew it. During his college days, he had taken a course in plant breeding that Hayes taught in which the professor preached the prevailing dogma that crops must be bred for specific locations, "and plant breeders must work in the place where their crop will be grown."

As Borlaug sat facing the committee, his plan met opposition: Sonora was a long way from the base of operations, and it didn't need as much assistance as the Bajio did.

Still, Norm was adamant: "I tell you, what happens in the valley in Sonora is important to the entire wheat program; it will point the way for all Mexico. I want the authority to delegate a good share of our effort to that region. And I want to do it in the way I think best."

Harrar said, "Goddammit, Norm, this scheme of yours has been considered twice, at your insistence, and voted down twice. Why can't you accept that?"

Harrar's abrupt dismissal sparked a fuse. Borlaug said, "If this is a firm decision, I also make a firm decision. You will have to find someone else to conform to your rules."

Stakman broke in: "Now, Norman, don't go jumping the gun."

Norm continued: "I have a couple of more things to say. You're laying down a policy that is wrong, and I can't go along with it. As of now, I resign. You'll have it in writing first thing tomorrow." He left the room.

At 6:30 the next morning, Borlaug went to his office. Stakman, who had never been known to be up that early, was there waiting for him, smoking his pipe. Stakman rebuked him for flying off the handle the day before. After some discussion, he convinced Norm to wait until later that day to write his resignation.

By coincidence, that very day Harrar received a letter from a prominent and respected farmer from Sonora whose land was adjacent to the Yaqui experimental station. The letter expressed admiration for the Rockefeller Foundation and for its mission in Mexico:

"For the first time, Dr. Harrar, I have seen a man come here from the Rockefeller Foundation or any other organization to help the farmer. Perhaps it is the first time in the history of Mexico that any scientist tried to help our farmers—I don't know that. The results are already evident in my own land with this new, wonderful wheat. I thank you, and I thank Dr. Borlaug...I want to say what is happening here with Dr. Borlaug will have a tremendous effect within a short time."

Stakman, who was convinced that Borlaug was right, intervened with Harrar that day. The letter from Sonora undoubtedly also had made an impression. When Borlaug came back to the office from a day at the Chapingo station, Stakman and Harrar were waiting. Stakman smiled. Harrar stood up, shook hands with Norm and said the matter had been reconsidered. Norm now had Harrar's official approval of the shuttle-breeding plan.

That fall, for winter planting at the Yaqui Valley station, Norm freighted two bags of seed of the newest varieties from the breeding program plus thousands of other promising lines and flew to Ciudad Obregon to supervise.

The shuttle-breeding process yielded a double bonus. First, as Norm had predicted, they were able to advance the generations twice as fast. The second result, even more important, was fortuitous. As the segregating populations were shuttled back and forth over ten degrees of latitude and from near sea level at the Yaqui Valley in Sonora to over eight thousand feet of altitude at Toluca, they were exposed to different diseases, different soils, different climates and different day-lengths: shortening from the time of planting in winter in Sonora and lengthening in summer in Toluca. The result was much more than simply a speeding of the breeding process. The plants that survived and performed well at both locations were now well adapted to a wide range of conditions.

Norm said, "The Princess of Serendip had smiled on our unorthodox shuttle-breeding effort."[18] It soon became apparent that these new early-maturing, rust-resistant varieties were broadly adapted to many latitudes and elevations in Mexico. Shuttle breeding subsequently gained credence worldwide as a method that reduced by half the years required to breed a new variety as well as for rapidly achieving wide adaptability to a range of variables.

Borlaug says, "Through the use of this technique, we developed high-yielding, day-length-insensitive varieties with a wide range of ecologic adoption and a broad spectrum of disease resistance—a new combination of uniquely valuable characters in wheat varieties."

These characters were valuable in increasing wheat production in Mexico and neighboring countries, including parts of the USA, but were to prove even more valuable a decade later when the widely adapted dwarf Mexican varieties were successfully introduced into Pakistan, India, Turkey, Egypt, Iran and China. Without this combination of characters, the successful transplantation of the Mexican varieties into other countries would have been impossible. And the Green Revolution might never have happened.

Third Innovation: Changing the Wheat Plant's Architecture

Mexico's wheat varieties were naturally slender and inclined to be tall. None of the varieties was capable of efficiently using heavy applications of fertilizer to increase yields. When fertilized they grew tall and rank; with wind at the time of irrigation or with rain they fell flat on the ground. Thus, more fertilizer often meant less grain per hectare. As the use of fertilizer increased and yields climbed to 4,500 kilos per hectare, lodging—the tall wheat plants heavy with grain falling over before ripening—began to limit further increases in yields. Borlaug began a search for wheat from different areas of the world to locate a suitable source of genetic dwarfness to overcome this barrier. He grew more than 20,000 lines, but found none with short, strong stems.

In late 1952, Dr. Orville Vogel, a prominent US Department of Agriculture wheat breeder stationed at Washington State University, had obtained preliminary successes in crossing a Japanese dwarf winter-habit wheat with his tall US winter wheats. Vogel had obtained a sample of the Japanese dwarf wheat seed—Norin 10—from a USDA agricultural advisor who was serving in Japan after World War II. The advisor had sent the seeds back to the USDA, which distributed them to several American wheat scientists, including Vogel, in 1948.

When Borlaug learned about these short-strawed wheats, he embarked on a third major innovation. In 1953, he obtained a few seeds from Vogel's most successful lines and began crossing them with the most promising, broadly adapted Mexican varieties. A new type of wheat—short and stiff-strawed instead of tall and slender—began to emerge. The progeny of the Japanese short wheat tillered profusely, thrusting up more stems from the base of the plant than western wheats, and it had more grains per head. A series of crosses and re-crosses gave rise to a group of so-called dwarf Mexican wheat varieties. The potential yield of the new varieties, under ideal conditions, increased from the previous high of 4,500 kilos per hectare to 9,000 kilos per hectare.

Dwarf wheat compared with the earlier tall wheat.

When former Governor Rodolfo Calles saw the results of Borlaug's research on wheat, he took the initiative to get land for a new station in Sonora. Norm says, "Don Rodolfo then organized farmers' groups, protected them from bureaucrats, and changed everything for the better."

The dwarf Mexican wheats were first distributed in Mexico

in 1961 and the best farmers began to harvest five, six, seven, and even eight tons per hectare. Within seven years, the national average yields had doubled. Borlaug named two of the best strains Sonora 64 and Lerma Rojo 64. It was these same dwarf Mexican wheats derived from the early days of Borlaug's transformative efforts that would later serve as catalysts to trigger the Green Revolution in India and Pakistan.

Borlaug's remarkable achievement in so few years was rare. Advances in agriculture typically are gradual. In describing the event, Don Paarlberg, who at the time was Director of Agricultural Economics in the office of the Secretary, US Department of Agriculture, wrote:

Don Rodolfo Calles and Borlaug admiring an early variety of dwarf Mexican wheat.

"Several things about this breakthrough made it special, gave it particular significance. It came in the hungry part of the world, not in those countries already surfeited with agricultural output. It came in the semi-tropics, which had long been in agricultural torpor, not in the temperate climates, where change was already occurring at a pace more rapid than could readily be assimilated. It produced new knowledge and technology that could be used by farmers in small tracts of land, rather than being, like many technological changes, adaptable only on large farms. And it was a breakthrough that came voluntarily, up from the grass roots, rather than being imposed arbitrarily from above."[19]

Borlaug had developed forty new rust-resistant, high-yielding tall varieties that made Mexico self-sufficient in wheat by 1956. By the early 1960s, thousands of strains of wheat had been crossed and the dwarf offspring were growing on the experimental plots. Important visitors from many countries appeared regularly to see the now-famous wheat station in Ciudad Obregon, Sonora, Mexico.

1950: Borlaug's bird-boy scarecrows, some of whom became famous technicians in CIMMYT's 1965-2000 team and contributed greatly to developing the technology that gave rise to the Green Revolution.

Borlaug is proud of the research station's "superintendent," Reyes Vega.

Borlaug hired Mexican boys as "bird watchers," to scare birds away from wheat research plots. Most of them could not read or write. He trained some of the boys to do technical tasks. Many became valued employees. Norm is especially proud of Reyes Vega, who on his own came up with a technique to increase by ten- to twenty-fold the efficiency of pollinating wheat plants. Norm says, "Then we commissioned Reyes as 'superintendent' of the research center, with responsibility for preparing land for planting. During harvest, Reyes labeled the breeding materials. He became a master technician."

Borlaug's team of young Mexican scientists and technicians in the Office of Special Studies worked hard. In a single season, the crew made from two to six thousand individual crosses. They developed techniques that reduced the time and cost of producing new crosses. Each year they studied the performance of some forty thousand varieties and lines, in various stages of development, most of which were planted in several locations.

Paarlberg says, "Planted end-to-end, his rows of wheat would have stretched four hundred miles!"

Borlaug and his Mexican colleagues analyzed these tests carefully. "Some of these kernels may be gold nuggets," he exclaimed. "Find them!" To find them was a case of meticulous selection and ruthless discarding. In twenty years of work, they created and distributed some seventy-five new varieties, of which four subsequently comprised the bulk of the wheat grown in Mexico, in much of the Middle East and in Latin American countries.

In 1967, in describing Norm and his work, his colleagues wrote, "And Borlaug did things. Dedicating himself to the cause of more bread for more Mexicans, he lived with wheat and absorbed a vast knowledge about it by fraternizing with thousands of kinds, from the seedbed to the seedbin. Work was not just a word to him; it became a code of honor. If genius is 'an infinite capacity for taking pains,' Borlaug had it, and so he worked day in and day out, from sunup to sundown, in the heat and dust and wind and rain—always in the fields and experimental plots or laboratories.... Borlaug's fanatical devotion to wheat paid big dividends. Many of his young Mexican associates caught the 'wheat fever' from him, and together they carried the wheat revolution to a successful conclusion."[20]

Borlaug with in-service trainees from several countries.

The rest of North America also benefited from the work of Norman Borlaug and his Mexican colleagues. In the early 1950s, a new race of the shifty stem-rust disease—named 15-B—devastated wheat fields in the Great Plains of the Upper Midwest and Canada. All the commercial wheat varieties of both the USA and Canada were susceptible to this new race.

Rust spores from the northern areas were carried south by the winds in the early fall and infected susceptible green fields of wheat in the southern US and Mexico, where they over-wintered. Then, in the spring, winds carried the spores back north to infect the wheat crops there. Severe epidemics in some areas of the Northern Great Plains occurred from 1950 to 1954.

More than 300 million bushels of wheat were destroyed in the USA in 1954 alone. That year, 15-B destroyed 80 percent of the crop of US durum wheat, used in macaroni and spaghetti products, and 120 million bushels of wheat in Canada. Borlaug says, "If a rust outbreak similar to the one in 1950-1954 had occurred in the US during World War II, we would not have been able to provide food for Europe. The outcome of the war might have been vastly different."

Severe losses from the 15-B epidemics stimulated an international cooperative effort to speed development of urgently needed rust-resistant wheat for North America. The US Department of Agriculture offered materials from their world wheat collection. Breeding lines from Canada, the USA, and the Mexican breeding programs were included. Borlaug recognized the potential of collaboration and in 1958 initiated the International Spring Wheat Yield Nursery that was grown in many areas throughout the world.

Reflecting on the experience years later, Borlaug wrote, "This nursery was the vehicle through which the broadly-adapted, high-yield, stem-rust-resistant dwarf wheat varieties spread around the world from Mexico. In fact, the introduction of stem-rust-resistant varieties by way of the International Spring Wheat Yield Nursery was instrumental in establishing the so-called Green Revolution in the Asian countries."[21]

As head of the US-based Rust Prevention Association, Dr. Don Fletcher, a protégé of E.C. Stakman, organized a cooperative research and seed increase program at Obregon where US and Canadian scientists could grow a generation of their breeding materials each winter in the Yaqui Valley. This greatly accelerated the release in the US and Canada of new varieties resistant to 15-B. The cooperative effort in collaboration with Norman Borlaug continued for twenty-seven years.

Dr. Eugene Hayden, still another of Stakman's protégés, was Fletcher's assistant and eventual successor. He said, "Starting in 1956, I made visits to Mexico twice each year for more than ten years to seed and harvest the International Grain Plots supervised by the Rust Prevention Association[22] for the US and Canada departments of agriculture. I was privileged to recognize Norm's genius before the world knew him."

Collaboration between the Rust Prevention Association and the Mexican program did indeed serve North America well. But as we shall see, this model of cooperation was the prototype for a more widespread international testing program that flourished from about 1961 through the 1980s and kept the shifty rust disease at bay.

Almost concurrently with adoption of the Mexican wheats came the increase in the new "miracle rice" produced at the International Rice Research Institute at Los Baños in the Philippines. Like the new wheats, the new rices were short-strawed, capable of standing erect when heavily fertilized, voracious feeders, widely adapted, and high-yielding. The techniques for developing the miracle rice were modeled in part on those used by Borlaug on wheat.

While positive results were showing in both corn and wheat production in Mexico, at least as important were the results of the training program. An intensive intern-training component was an integral part of the research program, targeting a new generation of Mexican scientists even as they were assisting with the research program. Fellowships were provided to enable the most promising of these young scientists to study outside the country for advanced degrees to prepare them for positions of leadership in Mexican agriculture, since there were no graduate schools in agricultural sciences anywhere in Latin America until 1959.

Dr. Borlaug with Dr. Evangelina Villegas, CIMMYT Cereal Chemist, and Dr. Arturo Hernandez, 'From bird-scare crow' to master technical to Ph.D. in Plant Breeding (Univ. of Minnesota).

In a lecture at Oberlin College in 1953, George Harrar said, "Many of the young Mexican scientists who have been associated with this program have now had training both in Mexico and abroad through Rockefeller Foundation scholarships and have returned to Mexico to accept positions of responsibility in the fields of agricultural research, education, and extension."[23]

One of the outstanding young Mexican scientists was Ignacio Narvaez, whom Borlaug met in his travels looking at wheat in the countryside. Nacho spoke some English and introduced Norm to farmers. They became close friends. One day Borlaug said, "Nacho, how would you like to join us—come down to Mexico City and work with our group in the Office of Special Studies?"

Narvaez jumped at the chance and said, "Dr. Borlaug, I am very proud you have asked me to join you." Nacho joined the program and after two years of experience in the wheat program was sent to the States to study, earned a Ph.D. at Purdue University, and became Norm's right-hand man in Mexico and later in Pakistan.

Borlaug became an advocate of those he had trained. "Give the young fellows a chance" was part of his basic code. In 1959, he said, "Nacho could run this Mexican wheat program as well as I can." He recommended Nacho—Dr. Ignacio Narvaez—for the job and Nacho got it.[24] In his history of the Rockefeller Foundation's early years in Mexico, E.C. Stakman wrote, "The development of a competent corps of Mexican agricultural scientists and scholars was the most valuable permanent contribution of the revolution in agriculture."[25]

Between 1943 and 1963, five hundred fifty interns participated in the Office of Special Studies agricultural research and training program in Mexico. Of these about two hundred received Master of Science degrees and about thirty the Doctor of Philosophy degree while on fellowships for study abroad. The Rockefeller Foundation "had worked itself out of a job," which was one of its original objectives.

In 1947, George Harrar hired Dr. John Niederhauser, a plant pathologist whose specialty was potatoes. In a few years, Niederhauser developed a control for potato late blight, the disease that caused the Irish potato famine in the 1840s. Under his guidance from 1950 to 1980, Mexico increased potato production six-fold. From his base in Mexico, Niederhauser helped foster strong national potato programs in other regions of the world. Several of the countries not only doubled their potato acreage, but doubled or tripled productivity, and the total national output increased by four to eight times. More than 180 scientists, from national programs all over the world, came to Mexico to learn potato production technology in the field, working with Niederhauser and his Mexican colleagues.

Niederhauser's success with potatoes led to creation of the International Potato Center (CIP) located in Peru in 1971. At that time, as a Rockefeller Foundation consultant, Niederhauser took a leadership role in establishing and managing this international center. He is given much credit for making the potato into the fourth most important staple food crop in the world in the twentieth century.

Borlaug was spectacularly successful in developing strains of high-yielding, short-strawed, disease-resistant wheat. Positive results in the maize program as well caused Rockefeller Foundation decision-makers to think about broader applications of the results. In the early 1960s, they began a transition from their national program in Mexico to an international program.

The transition for the maize breeding program to one of international scope was largely the work of Ed Wellhausen, who had been appointed director of the Mexican project when George

Harrar was called to Rockefeller's New York headquarters. From the base in Mexico, Wellhausen and his colleagues began moving maize germplasm around the world. Maize was a dominant cereal in much of Latin America and sub-Saharan Africa, as it was in North America.

In Asia, though, wheat and rice were the main cereals. In 1961, Borlaug began collaborating with agricultural scientists in selected other countries. With a goal of relieving their widespread hunger, he put high priority on India and Pakistan in his initial international efforts.

Meanwhile, Henry Wallace had made periodic visits to Mexico as an interested private citizen. He and Norm Borlaug became close friends. On one of those early trips, at the end of August 1948, at the personal invitation of President Avila Camacho, Wallace attended ceremonies marking the end of Camacho's six-year term. The highlight of his trip was a visit to the international experiment station founded at his suggestion by the Rockefeller Foundation. There he met Norman Borlaug and Ed Wellhausen and was amazed to see corn that would go more than seventy bushels to the acre.[26]

On another occasion, Wallace expressed interest in the new semi-dwarf wheats and their potential to revolutionize production in Asia. In 1963, at a celebration of the 50th anniversary of the founding of the Rockefeller Foundation, he said to Borlaug, "Are your new wheats going to make a difference in Asia?"

Borlaug boldly responded, "Give us five years and South Asia will be self-sufficient in wheat production."

As it turned out, this milestone was reached in 1968 in Pakistan and in 1972 in India. Borlaug says, "Sadly, Wallace died in 1965 so he did not live to see this happen."

Both Norman Borlaug and The Rockefeller Foundation credit Henry Wallace as the inspiration for the Green Revolution.[27]

Chapter Five

Rockefeller's Mexico Program Goes International

"In establishing the international centers The Rockefeller Foundation and The Ford Foundation complemented one another as could happen only with two private, completely independent non-governmental organizations willing to take the risks inherent in trying something new that had not been done before."

—Lowell S. Hardin

When Mexico became self-sufficient in cereals in 1956, the Rockefeller Foundation team had worked itself out of a job. By the late 1950s, the cooperative program had made such a contribution to Mexico's food production that leadership of the national wheat program was turned over to Mexican scientists and the Rockefeller team began thinking of ways to extend its important results to other countries.

Dr. Borlaug said, "Meanwhile, I was exploring the possibility of joining the research staff of a tropical fruit company to work on diseases of banana." While this was under negotiation, in early

1960, the Food and Agriculture Organization of the United Nations (FAO) and the Rockefeller Foundation formed a delegation to study wheat production problems across North African and Middle Eastern countries, from Tunisia to India. Norm joined the delegation and made his first trip outside the Americas, beginning the broader international phase of his life and work.

Under the UN flag, the team traveled through Algeria, Tunisia, Libya, Egypt, Jordan, Lebanon, Syria, Turkey, Iraq, Iran, Afghanistan, Pakistan and India. In each place they visited agriculture ministries, experiment stations and universities, observing wheat and barley research programs. One objective was to assess whether the high-yielding Mexican varieties might be useful for increasing wheat production in parts of this vast region. Norm saw areas where the Mexican wheat research information and varieties might well have a role.

Upon returning to Rome after the delegation visited countries in the region, Dr. Borlaug mused on the situation he had seen. Half of humanity was going to bed hungry. Many of the countries had virtually no agricultural scientists, but even in those that did the local scientists who were being paid to do something about the food situation weren't fired up about it. Norm recalls, "They were government servants with secure jobs and little incentive to address farmers' problems. In many cases they couldn't even recognize farmers' most important problems."

Borlaug concluded that the same program of training that had helped so many young scientists from Mexico and other Latin American countries to assume leadership in their countries' agriculture could be used to train and motivate young scientists from the Middle East and South Asia. In a report submitted to FAO in May 1960, Borlaug proposed a hands-on apprenticeship-type program to be established in Mexico to train young North African and Asian wheat scientists. The candidates were to be selected by FAO with financing by the Rockefeller Foundation.[28]

Borlaug's proposal was accepted. The first group of trainees arrived in Mexico in January 1961. Norm volunteered to handle the program to train the young scientists, not by discipline but across all relevant disciplines. This included genetics and plant breeding, agronomy, irrigation, plant pathology, entomology, and cereal technology. Trainees toiled in the fields twelve hours a day, from early February through April in Sonora and from May to October in Toluca and Chapingo, going through two wheat-crop cycles. They leveled and laid out sample plots, sowed the crops, and applied water and fertilizer—they got their basic training on the front lines in the battle against hunger.

Borlaug's report to FAO also proposed establishing International Spring Wheat Yield Nurseries to be widely grown in North Africa, the Middle East, South Asia and ten Latin American countries. Later, Canada, Australia and the U.S. were added. The nurseries were to include the main commercial spring wheat varieties from the region as well as the best varieties from Mexico, the US, Canada and South America. In coordination with the FAO Cairo office, Norm volunteered to supervise the preparation and shipment of seed for the nurseries. It became an integral part of the FAO-Rockefeller Foundation Mexican training program.

Wheat yield nursery, testing different varieties.

The first year, yield tests containing fifty varieties and breeding lines were planted at twenty-five locations. Each year more and more people wanted to grow the test. In the second year, the yield nursery was grown at fifty locations, then at more than one hundred. Eventually the best twenty-five wheats were sent for yield evaluation to one hundred fifty locations worldwide.[29]

Within three years, the yield and disease data from the international nurseries—much of it provided by trainees who had studied in Mexico but were then back in their own countries growing these nurseries—had clearly established the broad adaptation and good rust resistance of the Mexican semi-dwarf varieties. As the hunger crisis worsened, Pakistan in 1962 and India in 1964 began seriously to evaluate the Mexican varieties together with the improved crop management practices that permitted the varieties to express their genetic yield potential. Data from the International Spring Wheat Yield Nursery provided much of the information that made it possible to launch an aggressive crop production campaign in Pakistan and India in 1965 and 1966.

In the summer of 1963, Mexican President Adolfo Lopez Mateos made a trip to Southeast Asia and while in the Philippines, he visited the newly inaugurated International Rice Research Institute. When he asked about IRRI's origin, Robert Chandler, the director general, replied that it drew its inspiration from the Rockefeller Foundation program in Mexico.

Lopez Mateos was so excited by what he saw that on his return to Mexico he arranged a state dinner at which he thanked Harrar, Wellhausen, Borlaug and Niederhauser for their devoted work. The next day he met with George Harrar, who by that time had become president of the Rockefeller Foundation, and suggested that something like IRRI could be established in Mexico. It would focus on corn and wheat and become the vehicle for taking what had been learned and projecting from Mexico to the rest of the developing world.[30]

Dr. Robert Chandler explaining IRRI's origin to Mexico's president.

George Harrar discussed the concept with representatives of the Ford Foundation, who agreed to join with the Rockefeller Foundation to fund this international venture. On October 25, 1963, an agreement was signed with Mexico's Minister of Agriculture to establish the International Center for Maize and Wheat Improvement; in Spanish, the name is *El Centro International de Mejoramiento de Maiz y Trigo* (CIMMYT).

In 1966, CIMMYT was formally dedicated and an international board of trustees was established. Support for CIMMYT was initially from the Ford and Rockefeller foundations in collaboration with the government of Mexico. Additional financial support was soon provided by the US Agency for International Development (USAID), the United Nations Development Program (UNDP), and the Inter-American Development Bank (BID). Ed Wellhausen was appointed as the founding director of CIMMYT.

Lowell S. Hardin, formerly head of the Department of Agricultural Economics at Purdue, had been with the Ford Foundation less than a year when Sterling Wortman, Director of Agricultural Sciences at the Rockefeller Foundation, asked in 1966, "How would you like to be a founding trustee of CIMMYT?" Lowell said the answer was easy: "Ford and I agreed to say yes."

Later, Lowell said, "You will understand how great was my trepidation when you see who some of the people were who served on that board."[31] Among them were:

• J. George Harrar, USA, former resident director of the Rockefeller path-breaking agriculture program in Mexico and then the Foundation's president. (Lowell wrote, "If there had been a World Food Prize in his day George Harrar surely would have received it.")

• Virgilio Barco, Colombia, who was to become his country's ambassador to the United States and subsequently would serve as president of Colombia.

• Galo Plaza, Ecuador's minister of agriculture, then president of Ecuador, and later president of the Organization of American States (OAS), with headquarters in Washington, DC.

• Carlos P. Romulo, famous Philippine general, diplomat and political leader who shared military honors with General Douglas MacArthur, and became his country's ambassador to the US, having earlier been president of the General Assembly of the United Nations.

• Shri C. Subramaniam, India's Minister of Food and Agriculture.

• Prince M.C. Chakrabandhu, Thailand, an influential member of the royal family who had advanced training in agriculture.

• Emelio Gutierrez Roldan and Nichiolas Sanchez Duran, Mexico, senior agricultural scientists.

CIMMYT was born in the midst, and was largely a consequence, of the world crisis in food production—centered in

Asia—during the 1960s. Countries lacked foreign exchange to purchase food imports. Dire predictions were being made that without perpetual food aid many Asian countries faced continuing and worsening famines. Political leaders, many with their backs against the wall, became receptive to the then-radical advice of a handful of scientists who argued forcefully for the introduction of the new high-yield wheat and rice technologies developed in Mexico and the Philippines.

When the Rockefeller and Ford foundations in cooperation with the Mexican government established CIMMYT as an autonomous international training institute with an international board of trustees and staff, Dr. Borlaug was made director of its International Wheat Improvement Program. In this capacity he was able to realize more fully his objective of training young scientists in research and production methods. With CIMMYT's three research stations—one each at Chapingo and Toluca in the south and one in the Yaqui Valley in the north—Borlaug's shuttle-breeding research program would continue. The trustees stipulated that CIMMYT would make all its data and materials available worldwide, to any country, free of charge.

CIMMYT placed a very high priority on its efforts to develop training and leadership skills in support of collaborating national research institutions. Within twenty years, the center had some four thousand researchers from one hundred twenty countries as alumni of its in-service training courses and fellowship programs for visiting scientists, graduate students, and pre- and postdoctoral fellows.

Through the 1960s, Borlaug took dozens of scientists from South Asia under his wing. Some came to Mexico for formal training at CIMMYT, while many more learned from his visits to Asia. By the mid-1960s, the semi-dwarf Mexican wheats had won over the hearts of plant scientists in the region and were grown by progressive farmers, including many small farmers, in India and Pakistan.

Borlaug's new varieties were so popular in India that "when farmers saw the new wheats in the fields the demand for the seed was so great that guards with shotguns had to be stationed at the plots where the improved seed was being grown and multiplied. Otherwise it would have been stolen."[32] Black markets in Mexican wheat seed sprung up in both Pakistan and India by 1964 and 1965.

Robert Herdt, who was a Rockefeller Foundation senior agriculturist stationed in New Delhi, India at the time, tells the following story, which typifies Norman Borlaug's practical approach to teaching agricultural scientists.

"In February of 1967, Norm made a trip to India where, as was his practice, he visited the experimental plots at various places around the country. A new university had been established in the state of Uttar Pradesh at Pantnagar, about five hours' drive from Delhi, and scientists there had planted a trial with the wheats from Mexico, other international breeding lines, and crosses made by Indian scientists. Norm's visit was the occasion for gathering of local agriculturalists from much of North India, including some of us from the Rockefeller Foundation New Delhi Office.

"Scores of wheat varieties had been planted in small observation plots. The morning was cool but bright, one of those perfect late winter days in North India when the summer heat is still weeks away. Norm arrived with the university vice chancellor, the head of India's wheat program, and dozens of scientists trailing along. The field was a checkerboard of short, intermediate, and tall wheats, some beginning to mature and others still fairly green. Most looked healthy and many of the semi-dwarfs promised copious yields.

"Norm strode through the field barely glancing at one outstanding plot after another. He ignored the efforts of first one and then another proud scientist to explain the lineage of this or that line. Finally he found what he was looking for—a sorry, disease-infested plot of disreputable appearance. Pouncing on that plot he launched into a warning of the potential dangers of pride and complacency. At any time, new races of that 'shifty, changing, constantly evolving enemy,' wheat rust, could descend on South Asia and devastate entire regions, just as that unfortunate plot had been devastated. It was the job of wheat scientists to be ever alert to that possibility, to anticipate it, and to have breeding lines incorporating alternative sources of resistance ready, so if such a disaster threatened, seed could be multiplied and made available to farmers."

Herdt said, "Few of those attending could forget this lesson imparted by a gifted teacher with a burning mission."[33]

Chapter Six

Famine is Averted in India

"I wish I were now a member of India's Congress; I would stand up out-of-order every few minutes and shout in a loud voice: What India needs now is fertilizer, fertilizer, fertilizer, credit, credit, credit, and fair prices, fair prices, fair prices!"

—Norman Borlaug, March 29, 1967

Norman Borlaug had been spectacularly successful in Mexico in his scientific pursuits—developing high-yielding, short-strawed, disease-resistant wheats that were widely adaptable to a range of latitudes, elevations and soil types. To enhance the benefits of his scientific achievements he began adding the thoughts of a practical humanitarian:

How can we arrange to put the new cereal strains into extensive production in order to feed the hungry people of the world?

Can we achieve a temporary success in man's war against hunger and deprivation, thus creating a breathing space in which to deal with the "Population Monster" and the subsequent environmental and social ills that too often spark conflict between men and between nations?

With this self-imposed challenge, Dr. Borlaug started collaboration in 1961 with agricultural scientists in other countries, especially in India and Pakistan, where conditions for famine existed, and widespread starvation was a real prospect. India was a country trying to subsist with close to two and a half times as many people as there were in all of Latin America on a land area about one-fifteenth as large.

India had not sent trainees to Mexico for the first year of Borlaug's international training program. Pakistan had. Using seed that the trainees had taken home with them, Pakistan had been testing Mexican varieties for two years, and India had heard about it. In March 1963, the government of India invited Norm to come for discussions. A high-level luncheon meeting took place in the home of Ralph Cummings, Rockefeller Foundation's resident representative. Toward the end of the luncheon, Dr. M.S. Swaminathan, India's director of wheat research, said to Norm, "You've seen our program, do you think Mexican wheat can help us?"

Norm said, "If you really want to find out, if Dr. Cummings will arrange for me to stop in Pakistan and Egypt for two days each on my return to Mexico, I will get the results from my students who took seed from Mexico and have grown it for the past two years."

Arrangements were made. Pakistan organized a field day at Ayub Research Center at Lyallpur. Borlaug quickly surveyed the test plots in the nursery. Neither the Mexican nor the local varieties looked good; the care of the plots had been dismal.

Minister of Agriculture Malik Khuda Bakhsh Bucha, a colorful orator, held forth. Haldore Hanson, Ford Foundation representative, took notes. Pakistan's director of the Ayub Khan Research Center, Dr. Hossain, said, "Look, your Mexican wheats are no good."

Norm countered, "But you haven't used the right fertilizer, irrigation and weed control."

Hossain retorted, "Young man, this is the way we grow wheat in Pakistan!"

After everyone left, two Pakistanis—Manzoor Bajwa and M. Nur Chaudry—whom Norm had trained in Mexico and who had brought seed samples back with them, said, "We have something to show you; we'll pick you up before sunrise tomorrow."

At daylight, the two students took Norm to the far end of the experimental field and showed him four beautiful wheat plots. They had used Borlaug's recommended husbandry with their Mexican seeds. Norm said, "Why didn't you use these crop management practices to grow the plots in the main nursery?" They said, "The head scientists wouldn't let us use the technology that you had taught us. It's like you told us on the last day of our training in Mexico when you said, 'Don't try to change everything at once, they will slit your throat.' "

Norm told Hal Hanson about the students' plots, and then went on to Egypt where he experienced a similar situation. The Egyptian student—El Ham Talat—went through the same agony at the main nursery, but at his "private" plots at the sub-station, the result was very good. Norm asked, "Why is it that on the main station the wheat didn't do well?" The student said, "That's what you always told us in Mexico would happen..."

When Borlaug arrived at Sonora, Mexico three days later, he was swamped with the responsibility of harvesting. He hurriedly drafted a report about the excellent adoption of the Mexican dwarf wheats in both Pakistan and Egypt. He sent a rough draft of his report, "misspelled words and all," to Ralph Cummings and asked him to clean it up. In the draft Norm said, "In both Pakistan and India, there is too much chasing of academic butterflies." Cummings didn't tone it down.

When Hal Hanson received Norm's report, he said, "If your Mexican wheats look like a good bet here in Pakistan, the Ford Foundation will put some dollars into it."

In 1964 and 1965, India received five million tons of emergency wheat grain aid each year from the United States under the US government's Food for Peace program. Canada and Australia also sent grain. It was the largest food rescue operation in history. In spite of this, the famine worsened.

Malthusian thought—unchecked population growth always exceeds the growth of means of subsistence—was reawakening. Many biologists and economists were siding with Malthus.

Concern about the ability of the Earth to feed its people reached a crescendo with inadequate wheat crops, especially in India, in 1965, 1966 and 1967. Soon after taking office, President Richard Nixon instructed his Science Advisory Committee to study the world food problem. The Food and Agriculture Organization of the United Nations pushed its campaign against hunger.

The Paddock brothers, William and Paul, published a widely read book in 1967, *Famine 1975!: America's Decision; Who Will Survive?*, contending that famine on a vast scale was inevitable, and counseling that efforts to avert it be restricted to certain areas that promised some hope of success. India was written off as beyond hope.[34]

The following year, Paul Ehrlich published *The Population Bomb*. Writing as a biologist and environmentalist, his book was primarily about the world's rapidly growing populations and the need for "population control." But he also made predictions about food production, which he said could not possibly keep up with increases in human population.[35]

In 1967, even close associates of Norman Borlaug were not optimistic that food production would catch up in India. George Harrar, then president of The Rockefeller Foundation, and the person who had headed the expert team of Rockefeller scientists in Mexico from 1943 to 1952, said in an address in March of 1967:

"It is a fundamental fact that, next to world conflict, the greatest single threat to mankind is that of explosive population increase. To date, neither the disadvantaged countries nor those who would help them have been able to limit the vast increase in numbers."[36]

India and Pakistan were contributing more than their share to the population explosion, and had barely been meeting their food needs by importing increasing amounts of American wheat under the Food for Peace program. Nonetheless, the two countries wanted to improve their own food production rather than become permanent wards of the United States.

This was the climate of opinion in which Borlaug's new high-yielding Mexican wheats began to appear in the Asian subcontinent. The timing could not have been more propitious. As in the past, Borlaug's work seemed the product of benevolent destiny.

Borlaug arranged through the Rockefeller Foundation for Dr. Glenn Anderson, wheat expert and "gung ho leader" from the Canadian Department of Agriculture, to join the Rockefeller Foundation staff and help with the project in India. Dr. Ignacio Narvaez, native Mexican and one of Borlaug's earliest and most talented wheat apostles, was sent to Pakistan under a Ford Foundation grant.

In 1964, with help from the participants Norm had trained in Mexico, Borlaug's wheats were planted as experiments in various locations in both India and Pakistan. In 1965, in collaboration with local scientists and administrative officials, Borlaug arranged for 250 tons of seed of the Mexican dwarf wheat varieties to be imported into Pakistan and 200 tons to be imported into India for wide-scale testing on farms. Especially in those settings in which Norm's recommended cultural practices were followed, the on-farm trials yielded exceptionally well.

India's Minister of Food and Agriculture, Shri C. Subramaniam, said, "This wheat is better than anything we've ever seen. We'd better go with it."

Based on these promising results, supplemented with equally good results from the International Spring Wheat Yield Nursery that had been grown at many locations in the Near East, Borlaug concluded that it was time for strong production campaigns in both countries. But, to be successful, based on his experience in Mexico, he knew that the campaigns would have to be aggressive. The conventional wisdom at the time was that agricultural progress in developing countries would inevitably be slow. In 1967, the US President's Science Advisory Committee reported, "Since yield take-offs in the past have required educated, alert farmers, capital, and a commercial system of agriculture, they will be extremely difficult to achieve in the developing nations."[37]

But Norman Borlaug knew from his observations of the euphoric reactions to field trials of farmers in Pakistan and India that even small-scale peasant farmers would go with the exciting new technology if given a chance. A system was needed to provide participating farmers with a complete package of the new technology: the high-yielding seeds with instructions on when and how to plant, how to fertilize it, and how to manage weed and insect-pest control. As Norm saw it, that would be relatively easy compared with getting changes in government policies to make the campaigns a success.

Borlaug's grand scheme for the campaigns was what he called the "Kick-Off Approach," which he based on outright rejection of the hypothesis that agricultural development of necessity has to be slow. His Kick-Off Approach was founded on manipulating three factors—technical, psychological and economic—in such a way as to achieve rapid results. The technical factor had already been proved to his satisfaction in the results of the field trials. He now had to work on the psychological and economic factors to get the required policy changes.

Due to drought, late sowing and poor germination, India's spring harvest in 1966 from approximately three thousand hectares sown to Mexican wheat varieties, in half-acre plots on thousands of farms, produced mixed results. Many were good; a few were excellent. Borlaug, ever the optimist, said, "With superb handling of supplementary topdressing with nitrogen fertilizer and timely application of irrigation, the seedlings tillered profusely." And indeed in many locations yields were much better than any that had previously been recorded in India. Norm said, "The Lady of Serendip had smiled upon us, there was widespread enthusiasm, and euphoria reigned in a few locations."

At the time, the drought and famine were at their worst in northeast India, especially in Bihar and West Bengal.

Under these dismal conditions, Minister of Food and Agriculture Subramaniam made a courageous and historic decision. Against the advice of several of his senior scientists, he decided to import eighteen thousand tons of the short-strawed, high-yielding Lerma Rojo 64 seed from Mexico.

Borlaug (middle) coordinating India's large import of wheat seed from Mexico.

About the large import of seed, Norm says, "It unleashed a flood of criticism, because of the risks involved, from many academicians in ivory halls in affluent countries from around the world. Shri Subramaniam and I were charged by some critics with recklessly and irresponsibly playing with the lives of millions of people."[38]

In the fall of 1966, approximately 240,000 hectares were planted with seed of Mexican varieties. Before the plantings were made, a great controversy developed, with the economists from the Ministry of Agriculture, the Planning Commission, and the Rockefeller Foundation, including heavyweight David Hopper, on one side of the issue and Borlaug and Glenn Anderson on the other.

Norm recalls, "The economists insisted that we should cut back the fertilizer application from 120-40-0 kilograms per hectare of nutrients to 40-20-0 so that three times more area and families could share the benefit of fertilizer. We argued loudly and heatedly that this scale-back in fertilizer recommendations was premature, for we had not yet overcome the skepticism and psychological barrier of the traditionalists, peasant farmers, bureaucrats and senior scientists. At one point, the debate became both emotional and heated. With the diplomacy of Dr. Ralph Cummings, head of the Rockefeller Foundation team in India, we finally calmed down. We stood our ground and won the argument and the heavy rate of fertilizer was applied on 240,000 hectares." The dramatic results vindicated Borlaug and Anderson. The Mexican seeds were the catalyst. Fertilizer was the fuel.

Prime Minister Indira Gandhi lent her prestige to the wheat campaign by spading up the flowerbed in front of the Prime Minister's house and planting a plot of Mexican wheat, which developed beautifully and fulfilled its psychological purpose. Minister C. Subramaniam spaded up his cricket site and planted Mexican wheat. All professors in agricultural universities in the wheat belt were expected to plant a wheat demonstration plot employing the new technology in their front yards. Most did. Early in March

1968, after it was evident that the wheat crop would be a huge success, the Prime Minister issued a new postal stamp commemorating the Wheat Revolution.

Borlaug made a field trip during March 1967 with Drs. M.S. Swaminathan, S.P. Kohli and Glenn Anderson. Norm recalls, "I had an opportunity to observe many hundreds of farmers' fields throughout the wheat area. Euphoric wheat fever was widespread across the entire wheat-growing region. The grass roots were on fire! It had infected farmers, big and small, scientists, professors and politicians, and even a few immutable bureaucrats. The enthusiasm everywhere bordered on mania. I have never seen anywhere in agriculture such euphoria nor do I ever expect to see such reaction again."

This was vitally important because the government of India had not yet committed itself to an economic policy that would enduringly stimulate and permit the widespread adoption by small farmers of the package of new technology, as had been done a year before by the government of Pakistan.

While on the field trip, on March 29 Norm was asked to say a few words at a luncheon at the Escort Tractor Factory, at which some dignitaries and several members of the New Delhi press were present. "The Princess of Serendip smiled again and I seized the opportunity."[39]

Borlaug informed those present of the outstanding success of the wheat campaign and the enthusiasm of the farmers for the new wheats and the associated package of production technology. He closed by saying that if the government of India now would adopt an economic policy that would stimulate the adoption of the new technology, it could trigger a revolution in wheat production.

Borlaug indicated that government action was needed to assure (a) the availability of the right kind of fertilizer at reasonable prices at the village level six weeks before the onset of the planting season; (b) credit for the farmers to purchase fertilizer and seed before planting, to be paid back at harvest; and (c) an announcement before the initiation of the planting season that, at harvest, farmers would receive a fair price for their grain. He said the price should be similar to that of the international market rather than only half that price, as had prevailed for decades under the cheap food price policies that had prevailed since India's independence.

As a closing comment, Borlaug said, "I wish I were now a member of India's Congress; I would stand up out-of-order every few minutes and shout in a loud voice: **What India needs now is fertilizer, fertilizer, fertilizer, credit, credit, credit, and fair prices, fair prices, fair prices**!" Norm finished his talk by saying to the top official of the Escort Tractor Factory, "President Nanda, if the government makes the needed policy changes on fertilizer, credit and grain prices, the 250 unsold farm tractors in the 'patio' in front of your factory will be sold in one week, and you won't be able to catch up with orders for several years."

Afterward, Norm said, "There was a lot of chuckling. The press loved it."

The following morning, Borlaug and Anderson accompanied Dr. Swaminathan to pay respects to Prime Minister Indira Gandhi and President V. Giri and to inform them of the great success of the forthcoming harvest. Later they went to see the Minister of Agriculture and Food, Shri C. Subramaniam. They described the enthusiasm of farmers who had used or seen the new wheat production technology. They informed the minister of the bountiful harvest that was about to begin.

Norm says, "I bluntly added that with the grass roots on fire, unless fertilizer, credit and fair prices for grain at harvest were forthcoming soon, there would be trouble for the government. I explained that there were now perhaps several hundreds of thousands of farmers who knew what could be done if the government's economic policies were modified to permit it to happen."

Minister Subramaniam held up a handful of clippings from

that morning's New Delhi press quoting Borlaug's comments at the previous day's luncheon. Then he said, "I know what you are up to, but it is already too late for me. You have forgotten that I was so involved in the wheat program that I neglected to campaign adequately and lost my seat in the Lok Sabha [Congress] in the election of last month. I am out of office tomorrow night at midnight, so I cannot help the program anymore."

Then he continued, "I do believe your conclusions and, moreover, I want you to tell your story to the second most powerful man in the government, Mr. Ashok Mehta. He survived the disastrous Congress Party defeat last month. He is concurrently Deputy Prime Minister, Chairman of the Planning Commission, and Minister of Heavy Industry and Petro-Chemicals. He is in charge of fertilizer imports and fertilizer industry development."

Then the minister asked, "How long will you be in Delhi?"

Norm replied, "I leave for Mexico tomorrow night at midnight."

With that, the minister picked up the telephone and made an appointment for Borlaug and Swaminathan to see the Deputy Prime Minister the following afternoon at six.

Borlaug, Minister Subramaniam and Dr. Swaminathan, reminiscing thirty years later about the Green Revolution.

Norm recalls, "As we were leaving Minister Subramanian's office, I felt depressed and sad, realizing that the wheat campaign was losing the support of the official and friend who had done more than any other official to light the torch of the wheat revolution."

As they said goodbye, Minister Subramaniam said to Borlaug, "When you tell your story about the wheat program to Deputy Prime Minister Mehta tomorrow, don't pull any punches. Use the same blunt approach you have used on me when we were alone and when you wanted to provoke me to action. He needs to hear it straight from the shoulder."

The next afternoon, March 31, as Borlaug and Swaminathan were about to enter the Deputy Prime Minister's office, Norm said to his colleague, "I am going to follow Minister Subramaniam's suggestion and speak very bluntly to Minister Mehta about the government's disastrous policy on fertilizer, credit and grain prices. The meeting will very likely be stormy and I may be asked to leave the country, so you better keep a low profile. Should that happen, you and Dr. Anderson can keep the wheat revolution moving forward."

The meeting with Deputy Prime Minister Mehta proceeded quietly as Borlaug explained what was happening in the wheat revolution in many parts of the country. Norm emphasized that untold hundreds of thousands of farmers, small and large, had now seen what the new wheat technology could do to increase yields and farm income. An enthusiasm verging on euphoria seized all who had participated in the production campaign. Many more had seen the "miracle-like" technology and hoped to participate in the program next year.

Norm stressed that those hopes could not become reality for millions of small farmers until the government discarded its obsolete, ultra-conservative plans for rural development. He said the government needed to expand greatly the availability of fertilizer in the short-term from imports and in the intermediate-term from local production, and needed to increase the availability of credit to farmers to purchase fertilizer. Furthermore, the cheap food policy must be replaced with one that assured farmers a fair price for wheat at harvest—a price near that for wheat on the international market.

Borlaug stated, "Unless such a change in policy is forthcoming soon, the enthusiasm and expectations of hundreds of thousands of farmers will change to frustration and give rise to social and political disorder." Then he stated bluntly, "If this happens, you, Mr. Minister, will not occupy the position as Chairman of the Planning Commission, nor that of Deputy Prime Minister next year. Rather, you will be ousted, as has just happened to the Minister of Agriculture and Food. Moreover, the Congress Party will go down to defeat."

Minister Mehta reacted indignantly. Norm says, "For several minutes there was chaos with both of us talking in loud voices at the same time. A flood of loud angry words was emitted by both of us until we both ran out of breath and began to talk in rational tones once again."

Minister Mehta insisted that India did not have the foreign exchange to expand fertilizer imports, much less capital to invest in large fertilizer industry complexes. Norm countered that the development of a fertilizer industry was of a higher order of importance to the economy of the country than the large capital investments being made in certain other heavy industries, since fertilizer is essential for increasing food production.

Borlaug pressed on, "Moreover, it is a risk for India to continue to rely for a large amount of its essential food on imports under concessional sales through the US Food for Peace program. These concessional sales could be cut off either by unavailability or shortages by the supplier, or by shifts in political winds."

Several potential sources of funding were discussed: government of India, private Indian capital, private foreign capital, joint venture government of India and foreign governments, and the

World Bank. All of these were seemingly unacceptable to Minister Mehta.

Before leaving, Norm reiterated that he was fully convinced that if a new economic policy were to be adopted by government that would stimulate farmers to use the new production technology, there would be a much-needed surge in wheat production.

Norm says, "As the meeting ended, I think we had re-established mutual respect, if not mutual friendship."

Reflecting later about the meeting, Ex-Minister Subramaniam said, "The hour that Norman Borlaug spent with Deputy Prime Minister Mehta was probably the most productive hour of his career, for it apparently contributed to changing government policies on several fronts and greatly influenced agricultural production."

Norm left for Mexico four hours after the meeting. Two weeks later he received from offices of the Rockefeller and Ford foundations in New Delhi a series of clippings dated April 1st from all the major New Delhi newspapers. The clippings disclosed a drastic change in policies on fertilizer on two fronts: the government would begin to increase fertilizer imports for the short-term and would embark on a dynamic program to expand domestic fertilizer production. The subsequent increases in availability and use of fertilizer contributed to dramatic increases in food production.

Dr. Borlaug had apparently made his point well with Minister Mehta.

Borlaug says, "It is ironic that the next time Mr. Ashoka Mehta and I were to meet personally—about a decade later—was to discuss Indian wheat and rice surpluses, not deficits. Dr. Swaminathan, who by then had become Deputy Director of the Planning Commission, set up a meeting for me to discuss with Mr. Mehta the feasibility of using some of the surplus wheat grain to expand reforestation programs under the Indian government's new Food for Work Program.

"It was a cordial reunion under very different circumstances than those that had prevailed during the grain deficit of 1968."

In *The Population Bomb,* published in 1968, Paul Ehrlich had written that it was "a fantasy" that India would "ever" feed itself. By 1974, India was self-sufficient in the production of all cereals.

Chapter Seven

Father of the Green Revolution

"This new revolution can be as significant and as beneficial to mankind as the industrial revolution of a century and a half ago..."
—William S. Gaud

By the mid-1960s, Pakistan had been in existence as a sovereign nation barely two decades. Thanks to guidance from an elite cadre of civil servants trained by the British in London, buttressed by liberal coaching from the Harvard Advisory Group and Ford Foundation advisors, the new country was progressing generally quite well—with one important exception. Population growth was outstripping food supply. Pakistan was relying increasingly on food aid under the US Food for Peace program. Pakistan's citizens appreciated the donations, but they needed a permanent solution to their food problem.

In late 1965, as I sat comfortably in my plush office in the Federal Reserve Bank of Kansas City, I had a call from a recruiting officer in the US Agency for International Development, Department of State, in Washington, DC.

He said, "Chuck Elkinton, the Agricultural Attaché whom you worked with in Japan in 1960, is now director of USAID's technical assistance program for agriculture in Pakistan. He needs an experienced agricultural economist to serve as his understudy to help Pakistan increase food production. Would you be interested?"

I was.

Shortly after my arrival in Pakistan in early 1966, Elkinton was transferred to a position with broader responsibilities and I replaced him as chief of the agriculture division. We had a dozen well-trained American agricultural extension advisors. The problem was, we had too little to extend. We needed a shot in the arm—a catalyst.

Enter Norman Borlaug. What a breath of fresh air! He briefed me on the potential of the new wheat varieties, based on results of field-testing in Pakistan by the young scientists whom he had trained in Mexico. Then he said, "But you can't eat potential."

He explained that to achieve their potential, the Mexican varieties require heavy applications of fertilizer and a modification of farmers' cultural practices. Dr. Borlaug sought our help in training Pakistan's agricultural extension staff to teach farmers the proper techniques of growing the high-yielding varieties. As he left my office, he emphasized once again the importance of fertilizer and teaching farmers how to use it.

After the meeting with Dr. Borlaug, I spent about two months gathering information and interviewing key agricultural officials. Very few farmers used commercial fertilizer, but even those who did were using only miniscule amounts. I concluded that the existing system for distributing fertilizer to farmers—via the government's agricultural extension service—was inadequate to serve the needs of Borlaug's high-yielding varieties. I wrote a paper describing the situation and outlining a plan to transfer to the private sector the responsibility for fertilizer distribution.

USAID's Mission Director presented the paper to Pakistan's Minister of Development, who passed it to President Ayub

Khan, who said, "Let's do it."

And they did.

While Dr. Borlaug was briefing me, he mentioned that he and his colleagues at CIMMYT had developed a white-kernel variety, a cousin to the red-seeded Lerma Rojo 64, and noted that South Asians preferred white wheat. He said the white variety had not been released for commercial production in Mexico because it did not meet their bread-quality preferences. In any case, they only had a very small quantity of the seed.

Norm then told me this story to illustrate how politics can sometimes stifle progress. He said that because of a snowstorm in the US he had arrived a day later than planned for meetings with Pakistani officials and scientists. With no sleep and no time to rest, he was escorted by Haldore Hanson to a meeting in Lahore about Mexican wheats, chaired by a sub-secretary. Two Pakistani officials were trying to block the Mexican wheat program. Norm says they started out, "The Mexican wheats are the wrong color, taste bad, and they are too short-strawed; our cattle will starve because the wheat does not produce enough busa (forage)."

Norm countered, "You say they won't eat Mexican wheat because of the color. All wheat in the Asian subcontinent used to be red. The past two years, you imported close to ten million tons from the US plus some from Canada and a small amount from Australia. Your people apparently ate it. What color was the wheat from the US?"

Answer: "White."

"Wrong; it was all red."

"What color was the wheat from Canada?"

"White."

"Wrong; it was red."

"What color was the wheat from Australia?"

"Red, I guess."

"Wrong again; it was white. How do you explain?"

Norm says, "It was an awful meeting; everyone was mad.

Borlaug and Pakistan's Minister of Agriculture, Malik Khuda Bakhsh Bucha

After the meeting, Hal Hanson had a note from Minister Khuda Bakhsh Bucha inviting Hal and me to stop by his house for tea. Khuda Bakhsh, who was generally positive about the Mexican wheats, said, 'I hear they played rough.' "

In the process of gathering information after Borlaug's visit, I learned through an extended network that an enterprising private farmer in Mexico had somehow acquired some seed of the promising new variety, the white-kernel cousin to Lerma Rojo 64, and had proceeded surreptitiously to multiply it. West Pakistan's Secretary of Agriculture Amir Ahmed Khan asked whether it might be possible to acquire some of that seed. I wrote a justification for a $25,000 grant to procure 50 tons of the white seed from the Mexican farmer. The American ambassador, who had authority to approve grants of this size, signed off. Curry Brookshier, my deputy for what was then West Pakistan, called Staley Pitts, one of our American extension advisors who was on home leave in Arizona, and said, "Staley, get your ass down in Mexico and buy 50 tons of that new white wheat and get it over here in time to plant this fall."[40]

Staley was a no-nonsense, former football coach sort of guy. He flew to Mexico and negotiated with the farmer: "I'll give you a good price for 50 tons of this wheat delivered on the other side of the border in Arizona—you figure out how to get it over there." Staley knew better than to get tangled up with Mexican officials in moving illicit wheat across the border. The farmer agreed.

Staley christened the seed "MexiPak." The name stuck.

Staley arranged two semi-trailer grain trucks to be at the border to haul the seed wheat to the port at Los Angeles. Staley rode along. They arrived at the port on a weekend. An American-flag carrier was scheduled to depart LA on Sunday evening with Karachi as one of its intended ports. But no dockworkers were there on the weekend. Staley called the president of the line and said, "We've got people starving in Pakistan; you must help us."

Enough said. The wheat was loaded onto the ship before it departed Sunday evening.

When the wheat arrived at the port in Karachi, it was offloaded onto Army trucks, which fanned across the Punjab. Brookshier's agricultural extension staff distributed the seed in small packages to cooperating farmers, with instructions on how to plant and tend it to get maximum multiplication. The seed multiplied manifold and was distributed widely.

Pakistan learned that India had imported 18,000 tons of Mexican wheats in 1966. After their 1967 harvest, Pakistan sent their

Minister of Agriculture for East Pakistan to Mexico to purchase a large quantity of seed. Based on the experience with Staley Pitts' 50 tons, he especially wanted as much of the white wheat as he could get. The representative of northwest Mexico for the country's Minister of Agriculture had assembled thirty members of farmer cooperatives for a meeting in a small hotel. Officials of the cooperatives hoped to sell some of their red seed to Pakistan.

Norm says, "I introduced Pakistan's minister and started to leave. He said, 'No. You are my interpreter; you must stay. I don't speak any Spanish.'"

Norm was caught in the middle. He says, "The farmer who sold the illicit wheat to Staley Pitts was the main powerful person on the Mexican side. It was a tough set of negotiations. Pakistan's minister said, 'I will not buy any Lerma Rojo 64 or any other red-colored seed until I get 2,000 tons of the MexiPak white.' The farmer said, 'No, I only have a small amount.' The minister said, 'I cannot buy a ton of the red wheat until I get 2,000 tons of white.' The farmer finally said, 'Okay, 500 tons.' The minister said, 'No.' "

The representatives of all the farmer cooperatives were enraged at the farmer who held the trump card; they knew he had illegally obtained the "MexiPak" seed, and by refusing to sell 2,000 tons of it he was holding up the large sale of Lerma Rojo 64.

Bickering went on for nearly three hours. Finally, it got up to 1,700 tons of white and the farmer and Pakistan's minister made a deal. The farmer said, "Now, I only have a few tons for myself."

Norm says, "Then, in the next five minutes, Pakistan's minister bought 40,000 tons of the red-grained Lerma Rojo 64 from the farmer cooperatives, for a total of about 42,000 tons." Never before in the history of world agriculture, except for the 18,000 tons in India the year before, had more than 100 tons of seed of any grain crop been imported in one country from another, much less tens of thousands of tons.

The resulting yield from the 250 tons of seed that Pakistan had imported from Mexico in 1965 looked very promising indeed, in fields in which Borlaug's recommended husbandry had been followed. But Norm and his Ford Foundation colleagues in Pakistan were concerned that the government's economic policies provided insufficient incentive for farmers to make the needed investment in seed and fertilizer. And there likely would not be enough fertilizer for a major production campaign. Borlaug and his friends had convinced Minister Khuda Bakhsh of the need for policy changes, and the minister had successfully counseled the president.

In July 1966, President Ayub Khan made a bold economic policy decision. He committed his government to imports of fertilizer in the short-term and to investment in a domestic fertilizer industry. He pledged to provide credit to farmers for purchase of fertilizer and seed. And he called for drastic changes in pricing policy: the government would announce before the planting season that at harvest time farmers would receive a price for their grain equivalent to the price on the international market—not half that price as had previously been the case.

Dr. Ignacio Narvaez, who had been Borlaug's deputy in Mexico, was now Ford Foundation advisor on wheat production in Pakistan. With Nacho as coach, with Curry Brookshier's extension advisors on the front lines, and with a Ford Foundation-employed Norwegian economist—Dr. Oddvar Aresvik, consultant to Minister Khuda Bakhsh Bucha—sitting in an office adjacent to the minister's office, Pakistan launched a national wheat production campaign in the fall of 1966. The campaign was based on seed of the Mexican varieties that was harvested in Pakistan in April 1966, buttressed with Staley Pitts' 50 tons of MexiPak. The 1967 harvest from fields planted to the MexiPak seed was excellent.

During the second half of February and the early days of March 1968, when the crop was approaching maturity, Dr. Borlaug accompanied two Pakistani scientists and Nacho Narvaez to observe the wheat crop in all the important production areas.

Norm said, "The results we observed were startling. The crop was beautiful wherever the Mexican seed and improved technology were employed. An effervescent infectious enthusiasm prevailed among farmers, extension workers, research scientists and government officials everywhere. Even the immutable stolid bureaucrats were slightly infected by the virus of change."

Borlaug called on President Ayub Khan to brief him on his observations: "I'm just back from a trip through the countryside. The wheat crop is no longer in doubt, Mr. President. We have either reached or are close to reaching self-sufficiency. I am writing a report on the excellent crop; I will send it to Minister Khuda Bakhsh Bucha."

The President greeted Norm warmly, although he obviously lacked his usual luster. He said, "I'm very pleased to hear this, Dr. Borlaug, and I certainly appreciate your untiring effort in this great accomplishment. But you need to know, sir, that I am stepping down as president—I recently had a second heart attack. There will be an election to choose my successor. In the meantime, General Yahya Khan, my assistant, will be acting president starting tomorrow."

As Norm flew back to Mexico City, he was remorseful at the loss of support from Ayub Khan. Upon landing he finished his report and forwarded it to Khuda Bakhsh.

In mid-August, Borlaug had a telegram from General Yahya Khan. Norm says, "The acting president said, in effect, 'Get your ass over here—your report is causing us problems. I will be forced to import two million tons of wheat.'"

Borlaug flew to Islamabad right away. As he entered Yahya Khan's chamber, the general said, "The Green Revolution has failed. Wheat is not coming to markets. I need an explanation!"

Norm says, "Yahya Khan chewed me out—the worst chewing out I have ever had. He swore like a trooper." Norm laughed aloud when he said, "He must have been very much like our General Patton!"

When Yahya Khan finished, Norm said, "Sir, I can't be that far off, but let me check around and get back to you."

After again touring the countryside, Borlaug concluded that yields were indeed as high as he had earlier predicted. The problem was that, on the advice of economists, the government had dropped its guaranteed price for wheat by 25 percent. Speculators were hoarding the crop.

Norm reported loudly and clearly to the acting president, "The government is to blame! Reinstate the guaranteed price and the wheat will come rolling in."

He says, "Yahya Khan began replying in equally loud terms. But the price guarantee was restored and wheat flowed to the markets. There was no need for wheat grain imports."

The bountiful harvest of April 1968 brought Pakistan to self-sufficiency in wheat production.

Overruling the counsel of some skeptical local researchers, national leaders in India and Pakistan had taken calculated risks and, after widespread on-farm testing, decided to embark on major production programs to introduce the new seed/fertilizer technologies as quickly as possible. Once tens of thousands of farmers saw the yields of the new wheat and rice varieties grown using improved agronomic practices on demonstration plots on their own or neighbors' farms, they themselves became the major spokesmen for increased adoption. The spread of these new wheat and rice varieties is unparalleled in the history of agriculture, except perhaps for the spread of hybrid maize in the developed countries during the 1940s, 1950s, and 1960s.[41]

William S. Gaud, Administrator of the United States Agency for International Development, coined the phrase "The Green Revolution" on March 8, 1968, in an address before an international group in Washington, DC:

> . . . Developments in the field of agriculture contain the makings of a new revolution. It is not a violent Red Revolution like that of the Soviets, nor is it a White Revolution like that of the Shah of Iran. I call it the Green Revolution.[42]

In his address Bill Gaud said, "In May 1967, Pakistan harvested six hundred thousand acres that were planted to a new high-yielding wheat seed. This spring [1968] the farmers of Pakistan will harvest the new wheats from an estimated three and a half million acres. They will bring in a total wheat crop of seven and a half to eight million tons—a new record. Pakistan has an excellent chance of achieving self-sufficiency in food grains in another year."

As it turned out, Pakistan achieved self-sufficiency in wheat production with the harvest of April 1968.

Mr. Gaud continued: "In 1967 the new high-yielding wheats were harvested from seven hundred thousand acres in India. This year they will be planted to six million acres. Another ten million acres will be planted to high-yield varieties of rice, sorghum, and millet. India will harvest more than ninety-five million tons in food grains this year—again a record crop. She hopes to achieve self-sufficiency in food grains in another three or four years. …"

She did.

Gaud said, "Turkey has demonstrated that she can raise yields by two and three times with the new wheats. …The Philippines have harvested a record rice crop with only fourteen percent of their rice fields planted to new high-yielding seeds. … The Philippines are clearly about to achieve self-sufficiency in rice."

Other countries were beginning to show significant increases in cereal production by 1970, including Afghanistan, Ceylon, Indonesia, Iran, Kenya, Malaya, Morocco, Thailand, Tunisia, and Turkey.

A revolution was truly in the making.

Borlaug's Mexican dwarf wheat varieties and their Indian and Pakistani derivatives had been the principal catalyst in triggering the Green Revolution. The unusual breadth of geographic adaptation combined with high genetic yield potential, short straw, a strong responsiveness and high efficiency in the use of heavy doses of fertilizers, and a broad spectrum of disease resistance had made the Mexican dwarf varieties the biological bombshell that launched the Green Revolution.

During the 1969-1970 crop year, 55 percent of the six million hectares sown to wheat in Pakistan and 35 percent of the fourteen million hectares in India were sown to Mexican varieties or their derivatives. Never before in the history of agriculture had a transplantation of high-yielding varieties, coupled with an entirely new technology and strategy, been achieved on such a massive scale in so short a period of time with such great success.

Despite the tremendous production gains achieved in many developing countries in a very short time, Green Revolution technologies became the subject of intense controversy. Many initial reports depicted the new wheat and rice technologies as an ill-advised wholesale transfer of high-yield, temperate-zone farming systems to peasant farmers in the Third World.

Population doomsayers likened the Earth to a lifeboat that could only hold so many passengers without sinking. Moreover, they viewed international assistance efforts in agricultural research as an encouragement to greater population growth, which, as a result, would lead to a disaster of greater proportions later.[43]

Borlaug said, "Critics of our attempt to assist both India and Pakistan to improve their cereal production were numerous, scandalous, and demoralizing. They said we were recklessly playing with the lives of millions."

The critics comprised a broad spectrum, from academia to business to governmental organizations, from both the developed and developing nations. Some argued that there was no hope for saving overpopulated India; they advocated a system of classification based on population size and growth rate. This international triage would simply abandon those countries beyond salvation to starvation, lest in trying unsuccessfully to save them, other nations perhaps salvageable would also be lost.

Several outstanding scientists from developed nations claimed that the importation of the huge quantities of seed from Mexico was reckless and in fact was risking the lives of millions of innocent poor people. Some scientists, political leaders and bureaucrats in high positions within the governments of both India and Pakistan tried to scuttle the program.

But the poor and hungry people in South Asia had a different slant on the Green Revolution!

In the spring of 1968, I had word from Robert D. Havener, a Ford Foundation representative who was also living in Lahore, that a prestigious entourage was expected to cross over in a few days from India to Pakistan. The group included Norman Borlaug, E. C. Stakman, Forrest (Frosty) Hill, and Lowell S. Hardin.

As described earlier in this narrative, E. C. Stakman had been the Rockefeller Foundation's consultant who led the team in Mexico in the early 1940s to design the first foreign agricultural assistance program—a program that evolved two decades later to become CIMMYT. Thus, Dr. Stakman was the premier architect of what came to be an international network of agricultural research centers, one of the most powerful global institutional developments of the twentieth century.

Frosty Hill, who had grown up in a family of dry-land wheat farmers in Western Saskatchewan, was the Ford Foundation vice president for overseas operations. In the late 1950s, Frosty Hill and George Harrar of the Rockefeller Foundation had conceived the concept of the International Rice Research Institute (IRRI). Their model for IRRI was based to a large extent on the Rockefeller Foundation team's successful work in Mexico. IRRI was dedicated in 1960 and began operations in 1962 with joint foundation funding as the first international agricultural research center.

Lowell Hardin, as senior agriculturist in the International Division of the Ford Foundation, was a member of the founding Board of Trustees for CIMMYT, which was dedicated in 1966 as the second of the set of international agricultural research centers. My wife Florence and I had become well-acquainted with Lowell and his wife during the summer of 1960 when, at Lowell's request, I had assisted him in Japan for three months to do an evaluation of the US Food for Peace program in that country.

Florence and I asked Bob Havener, who was coordinating arrangements for the team's tour, whether we might host an open house to introduce the team to key Pakistani scientists and top-level government officials, including the colorful Minister of Agriculture, Malik Khuda Bakhsh Bucha. Bob agreed. Less than three years later, Florence and I could brag that we had opened our house to a Nobel Peace Prize laureate.

When the honored guests arrived for the open house, they described with excitement the exceptionally warm welcome that had been given to Borlaug by Pakistanis as the entourage crossed the border from India. Dr. Borlaug was becoming known locally as "Father of the Green Revolution."

But one of the greeters at the border carried a discouraging message. A farmer near Lyallpur had a field of MexiPak wheat that was "sick" with some kind of strange disease. The messenger asked Dr. Borlaug to please go with him to Lyallpur to see the sick wheat and diagnose it.

Fearing that it might be an outbreak of rust, one of Borlaug's persistent worries about the new wheat strains, he readily agreed to go and, undoubtedly, was more than a bit apprehensive during the one-hour road trip. When they arrived at the site of the "sick wheat" field, Norm was puzzled as he viewed one of the finest stands of MexiPak wheat he had ever seen. He was also puzzled that a sizeable group of Pakistanis were waiting patiently for him at the site, where a large carpet had been spread for the distinguished visitor.

The "sick wheat" story had been a hoax! The Pakistanis had concocted the story as a way to get Dr. Borlaug to come to the site and witness this miracle first-hand. But most of all, as a group they wanted to show their deep appreciation for what he had done to relieve their hunger.

Chapter Eight

Margaret Copes with Loneliness

"I had to take the good with the bad—being married to a great man."
—Margaret Gibson Borlaug

The Borlaugs enjoyed a happy and normal life while Norman was with DuPont in Wilmington. Their sparkling, vivacious Jeanie was pure joy. Even after they moved to Mexico, Norm was usually at home on weekends, although on his trips to the Yaqui he was sometimes away for a few weeks. Extending his work to South Asia meant that he was often gone for months at a time. Margaret was lonely, extremely so at times, but did not complain. She was always supportive of Norman and his work. But in terms of family life, the couple was paying a hefty price for Norm's exemplary successes.

In the early days in Mexico, Norman and Margaret were thoroughly enjoying Jeanie. At the same time, Norm yearned for

The Borlaug family in Mexico City.

a son. During the summer of 1946, Margaret informed Norman that she was expecting. They talked about whether she should return to the States for the birth. Margaret expressed a strong desire to remain in Mexico and assured Norman that she would be fine. On March 29, 1947, just four days after Norm's 33rd birthday, William Gibson Borlaug was born.

Dr. John Niederhauser had joined the Rockefeller team in 1947 as a scientist working to improve potato production. He and his wife had six sons and a daughter. Billy Borlaug grew up spending a lot of time with the Niederhauser family. In 1954, in an attempt to make spare time more meaningful for their children as well as a way for families to share times together, John and Norm started Little League baseball in Mexico City. Four local businesses initially sponsored the league. The first year, the majority of the players were from American families living in Mexico. Games were played at the American School baseball field in Mexico City. John and Norm each coached a team. Norm says, "I'd finish in the experimental fields Friday evening, make the six-hour drive to Mexico City, and coach my team on Saturday mornings."

He recalls, "The first year our scores were very high and games were not well played. But over time, the young players grew more sophisticated. The games became quite a social event. The next year we had four leagues: the Aztec, Maya, Toltec and Metropolitan leagues. By the second year, half the players were Mexican and by the third year, 95 percent were."

The Mexican Little League spread to Monterrey in 1956. Norm says, "In 1958, the Monterrey team won the Little League world championship in Williamsport, Pennsylvania."

Later, Norm was involved in organizing a Pony League and a Colt League for older, mostly former Little League players.

Bill Richardson, the current governor of New Mexico, grew up in Mexico City and participated in Little League, in the Maya League. Billy Borlaug was in the Aztec League. Later, they both played in Norm's Colt League team. Norm says, "Richardson was

Norman Borlaug coaching son Bill.

a better pitcher than Billy, so I always chose him to pitch when my team was in a tight spot in the playoffs."

When he was 14, son Bill, who was growing tall, strong and lanky, went off to prestigious Shattuck School, a prep school in Faribault, Minnesota, from which he graduated in 1965. He then went to the University of Oklahoma, where he received a B.S. degree in 1970. He earned an MBA degree from Thunderbird in 1972.

In the fall of 1963, just a year after Bill had left home, beautiful, intelligent and spunky Jeanie matriculated at the University of Kansas, where she majored in education. She was preparing to teach Spanish. Norm says, "Jeanie is a natural-born teacher."

Margaret Borlaug was often lonely after they moved to Mexico from Wilmington. By late 1963, with Norm's being away much of the time and the children both in the States, she suffered from empty-nest syndrome. To lessen the boredom, Margaret frequently flew to the States to visit Bill and Jeanie, or to spend time with Norman's family in Iowa or her sister in Kansas. Her mother and father had died several years earlier.

While she was at home in Mexico, Margaret read incessantly. She went on tours oriented to the history of Mexico City. This helped to improve her already respectable "kitchen Spanish." She served as a volunteer for several worthy causes, including with Girl Scouts, Cub Scouts and the American Society. She taught English to second and third graders in a private school for ten years.

Norm says, "One of the positive things about the time in Mexico was what I call the Rockefeller Foundation extended family. Every Saturday night—as well as on the Christmas, New Year, Thanksgiving and Fourth of July holidays—all the foundation scientists, their spouses and their children got together for a party. It was a very tight-knit group. They all looked out for each other. This is another place where Margaret shined. She knew all the children of the foundation families and often helped care for them."

Even with all these activities, Margaret confesses that she was lonely much of the time.

With the children now away from home and on their own, Norm and Margaret began thinking it was time they took an extended trip—just the two of them. They had had neither time nor money for a romantic trip at the time they were married. This would be their long-delayed honeymoon.

The trip would be an extension of a series of events. Norm had been asked to participate in meetings at FAO in Rome in early February 1967. Margaret had always been curious about her Scottish ancestry; she would spend a few days in Scotland in search of family relatives. The two would meet in Rome and then proceed to Pakistan and India, where Norm was to consult with government officials and scientists. From there, the couple would spend several days each in Bangkok, Hong Kong and Japan. From Japan, they would sail to San Francisco, stopping on the way in Hawaii for two or three days.

On the morning that Margaret arrived in Rome, Norm informed her that they must leave that night for Pakistan and India; he had received urgent messages requesting his counsel about South Asia's worsening hunger and famine situation. Many years later, Margaret told me, wryly, "I had half a day to see Rome. We went to the Sistine Chapel; that's all we had time for."

Norm says, "Those were busy times in India and Pakistan. India was suffering famine in two northeastern provinces. The government was debating at the highest levels the merits of a shift in policy to emphasize the new Mexican wheat technology. In that situation, I simply could not go off on a honeymoon. That would have to wait."

Margaret proceeded alone on "the honeymoon," chaperoned by a Rockefeller Foundation staff person.

Edwin J. Wellhausen, the first director general of CIMMYT, had become well acquainted with the Borlaugs while Norman was working in Mexico. In commenting years later on the family, he captured Margaret's role succinctly when he said, "Borlaug's beautiful, highly capable wife and great lady, Margaret, has contributed much to his success. She has supported him in every way. She has handled all domestic affairs and served as the family matriarch for years. She deserves much credit for the accomplishments and successes of her great husband."[44]

I had the rare privilege of visiting the Borlaug family in Dallas for four days in June 2005—Norman and Margaret, daughter Jeanie, son Bill, three of their five grandchildren, and all four of their great grandchildren. What a remarkable family! Among the many treasured moments was one in which Norm volunteered a crisp assessment of Margaret's role as a mother: "She left deep marks on Jeanie and Bill; she gave them worthy values, knowing right from wrong. She deserves most of the credit for how well they turned out."

Chapter Nine

The Birth of a Global Network of Research and Training

"Perhaps the most important contribution of all is that the methods and tactics used so successfully in making the production breakthrough in wheat, first in Mexico and then in India and Pakistan, served as a model for production programs with many other crops and in many other countries."

—Norman E. Borlaug

The Rockefeller Foundation had been chartered "to promote the well-being of mankind throughout the world." After the initial successes in agriculture in Latin America, it was time to take a look at the Far East.

On a pleasant day in the late 1950s, George Harrar of the Rockefeller Foundation and Forrest (Frosty) Hill, Vice President for Overseas Development of the Ford Foundation, sat at an outdoor café in Manila sipping coffee and brainstorming about an entirely new global concept—an international agricultural research center focused on ways to increase the production of

A portion of the CIMMYT experimental station. Compare this with the first station as shown in the picture on p. 37.

one crop—rice. They were seeking a way to short cut the time it would take individual countries to train qualified scientists to do research adequate to solve their hunger problems. Their model was the highly successful Rockefeller Foundation-sponsored collaborative research project in Mexico.

The rendezvous in Manila sprang from a chance discussion in August 1958 in which George Harrar was a luncheon guest at Ford Foundation's New York headquarters to discuss an unrelated project. Toward the end of that meeting, Frosty Hill turned to Harrar and said, "You know, George, someone should undertake to work with rice the way you Rockefeller Foundation people have with corn and wheat." Harrar replied that the Rockefeller Foundation had been concerned with the rice problem for some time. Then, referring to the two foundations, Hill said, "We have some money. You have experience in conducting agricultural research in the developing countries. We both are interested in doing what we can to help solve the world's food problem. Why don't we get together and see what we can do?"[45]

Continuing discussions resulted in the formation of the International Rice Research Institute (IRRI) in 1960. In a cooperative effort the government of the Philippines supplied the land and other facilities. The Ford Foundation supplied funds for the physical plant while the Rockefeller Foundation provided scientists and administered the program. IRRI was officially dedicated in 1962 to become the first international agricultural research center. The mission of the Institute, located at Los Banos on the island of Luzon, was to work exclusively on the region's all-important but too-long-neglected rice crop. Drawing on Norman Borlaug's successful model in wheat, the research staff would search for an improved rice variety of short stature that would be responsive to fertilizer and other improved crop management practices.

The Institute initially drew from the Latin America experience for some of its staff, but most of its trustees and the bulk of its scientific staff were distinguished officials and scientists from several countries of Asia. Dr. Robert F. Chandler, Jr., an eminent Rockefeller Foundation scientist, was appointed as the first director of IRRI, and Sterling Wortman, also a Rockefeller scientist, was designated assistant director. George Harrar was the first chairman of the Institute's board of trustees.

George Harrar was appointed in 1961 as the new president of the Rockefeller Foundation. Early in his tenure, he sought the support of the trustees of the Foundation to continue—even strengthen—its program aimed at improving global human nutrition. He lent his hand to the preparation of a report to the trustees, which they approved. In part, the report said:

> About half of the human beings on earth have an inadequate diet, and millions live constantly on the edge of starvation, despite the fact that an overabundance of food is produced in a few technologically advanced countries. A world that possesses the knowledge and methods to confront the demands of hunger must accelerate its efforts to increase the production and improve the distribution of food.
>
> We propose during the years ahead to strengthen that part of the foundation's program that is directed to human nutrition. This will mean increasing the quality and the quantity of those foods that feed the world. … It will involve the search for new knowledge leading to better use of land and water resources, development of non-conventional agricultural techniques, and investigation of the changing environment in which we live.[46]

When Bob Chandler was selected by its Board of Trustees as the founding director of the International Rice Research Institute, he knew whom he wanted as his senior rice scientist: Dr. Henry M. Beachell, known by his friends as Hank. Norman Borlaug says, "Hank Beachell grew up on a Nebraska farm, was educated at the University of Nebraska, was interested in all aspects of agriculture, and after a successful thirty-two-year career with the US Department of Agriculture stationed at Texas A&M University's Beaumont Research Center working as a rice breeder, was 'the old vet' of rice."

Hank Beachell accepted Bob Chandler's challenge.

In 1966, just four years after the research program got underway, IRRI released its first named rice variety, IR8—a plant of short stature with thick, sturdy stems that resisted lodging. IR8 was quickly adopted in the Indian sub-continent and elsewhere with dramatic results.

The rapid spread of IR8 throughout the rice-growing areas of Asia was the second half of the contribution of foundation-sponsored research to the Green Revolution— "miracle" rice to accompany "miracle" wheat. The progress of the research program at IRRI exceeded the expectations of both Harrar and Hill.[47]

An officer of the American Society of Agronomy, Dr. E.C.A. Runge of Texas A&M University, wrote that Hank Beachell is considered to be "the individual most responsible for the Green Revolution in rice. Like Borlaug on wheat, Hank was an agriculturist with interest and knowledge across all scientific disciplines related to rice research and productivity."

As indicated in Chapter Five, CIMMYT was dedicated in 1966 as the second international agricultural research center, with emphasis on maize and wheat.

It is proper that the first two centers focused on rice, maize and wheat. Of the seven thousand total plant species used in agriculture in the world, these three crops make up half of the world's plant-derived calorie intake. But other crops are also important—beans, lentils and cowpeas, for example, as sources of protein for people with modest incomes. Potatoes, cassava, sweet potatoes, and other crops and vegetables are important in many countries. And what about livestock?

The world took notice of the dramatic results from the first two centers. As the results became more widely known, the Rockefeller Foundation and other institutions were besieged by requests from many countries for assistance in agricultural improvement programs.

In 1967, two more international centers were authorized to stimulate production of certain tropical crops and animal species as well as to help train scientific specialists: the International Center of Tropical Agriculture (CIAT) in Colombia, and the International Institute of Tropical Agriculture (IITA) in Nigeria. CIAT was initially financed by the Ford, Rockefeller, and W. K. Kellogg foundations in cooperation with the government of Colombia. The Ford and Rockefeller foundations and the Canadian International Development Agency (CIDA) initially supported IITA in collaboration with the government of Nigeria.

These four international institutes represented a significant start toward the construction of a worldwide network of international, national, and local research and training centers.

Several regions of Africa, Asia, and Latin America began campaigns to have centers to do research on crops and livestock species that were important in their areas of the world. It was clear that the world needed still more centers, but the available funds of the two main partners—the Ford and Rockefeller foundations—in the formation of the first four centers were fully committed. A system was needed to analyze the requests for regional research services, including the needed funds to implement them.

A search for partners was launched. To facilitate that process, the first of what developed into a series of conferences was hosted by the Rockefeller Foundation in April 1969 at its stately retreat and conference center, the Villa Serbelloni on the shores of picturesque Lake Como, Bellagio, Italy.

In a history of the formation of the Consultative Group on International Agricultural Research, Warren Baum wrote, "The Bellagio Conference was a unique gathering of top officials of international, regional, national, and private organizations concerned with agriculture. It included the heads of three United Nations agencies (the FAO, the UNDP, and the World Bank), the heads of the US, Canadian, Swedish, and British aid organizations, and senior representatives of the Inter-American Development Bank, the Asian Development Bank, and the Japanese Ministry of Foreign Affairs. Both of the foundations were well represented by top officials. … The conference met against a background of worldwide concern, if not despair, over the problems of static food production and rising population in the developing world, mixed with a new hope that modern technology might offer an answer to this age-old problem."[48]

In his foreword to the published proceedings of the Bellagio conference, Will M. Myers, the chairman of the conference, wrote:

> In recent years, we have become increasingly aware that in the underdeveloped nations, most of which are predominantly agrarian, agricultural development must precede or at least be concomitant with industrial and other economic and social development. We now understand, better than in the past, that a modern industrialized society cannot be built on the quicksand of a traditional subsistence agriculture, particularly in nations where 75 to 85 percent of the people are engaged in agriculture. … If the developing nations are to catch up with the developed nations, they must make massive strides in increasing the productivity and efficiency of their agricultural sector. …

> [In some countries] the decline in per capita food production exacerbates an already serious situation.[49]

Lowell Hardin, who participated in the Bellagio conference, reports that ideas only began to coalesce when Frosty Hill, in a homespun and persuasive presentation, spoke about how the new varieties were transforming agriculture in places like India's Punjab. Thereafter, a consensus began to form about the importance for the international community to seize the opportunity afforded by the new technology.[50]

Hardin reported that in attendance at the Bellagio conference "were the high priests of agricultural development from the industrial nations, UN organizations, development banks and foundations." Among the "high priests" was Robert S. McNamara, who had been Defense Secretary under presidents Kennedy and Johnson and was now president of the World Bank.[51]

As part of the program, Bob Chandler, the no-nonsense founding director of IRRI, told his "miracle" rice story. The breeding programs which developed the "miracle" rices at IRRI and the "miracle" wheats at CIMMYT were remarkably productive research enterprises. Both involved the successful introduction of genes from dwarf varieties to produce crosses which had shorter, stiffer straws than their tall parents. These sturdy new plants were able to respond to heavy applications of fertilizer without lodging and falling over as invariably happened with the taller varieties. Under irrigation these new semi-dwarf rice and wheat varieties yielded two to three times as much grain per acre as the varieties they replaced. Little wonder that farmers and the press called them "miracle" varieties.

Hardin says, "When we showed rates of return on the investment in rice research of over 50 percent, McNamara edged forward in his chair and listened attentively. Then he stood up and made this promise: 'If you with your centers can generate returns like that, we'll help you raise the money you need.' " He did.

Before McNamara became president of the World Bank in April 1968, he had acquired considerable experience with applied research as president of the Ford Motor Company and as US Secretary of Defense. After coming to the bank he continued to serve as a director of the Ford Foundation, so he was familiar with its programs. Following the Bellagio Conference he launched a campaign to place the bank in the forefront of organizing the international funding of agricultural research.

At the September 1969 annual meeting of the World Bank's Board of Governors, McNamara said, "We should assume a greater role of leadership in promoting the agricultural research of today that will be the foundation of greater agricultural growth tomorrow."

In January 1971, a vice president of the World Bank said that support for international agricultural research "will ultimately prove to be the highest yielding investment we can make, in terms of increased production and greater momentum for development generally."

In the spring of 1971, just a few months after Norman Borlaug's award of the Nobel Peace Prize for alleviating hunger, the first of what later came to be known as "Centers' Week" was held in Washington, DC. Borlaug and Wellhausen were participants, as was Bob Chandler. Norm says, "More than 400 people from around the world attended subsequent Centers' Weeks, but this first one was an informal gathering of not more than 35 scientists and investors. International Center directors reviewed their recent work and progress and laid out their financial requirements for the coming year or years. Representatives from various donor organizations listened to the technical presentations and the financial needs of the Centers and made commitments in a spirit of trust and respect. Then everyone returned home and went to work."

Much of the impetus of the "spirit of trust and respect" undoubtedly stemmed from the 1970 Nobel Peace Prize having been awarded based on the dramatic impact of research that fostered the Green Revolution.

A series of Bellagio conferences resulted in 1972 in the formation of an informal sponsoring entity, the Consultative Group on International Agricultural Research (CGIAR), with headquarters at the World Bank in Washington, DC.

In early 1973, I was transferred from Pakistan to the State Department in Washington, DC, where for five years I was director of the US government's worldwide program to help developing countries increase their food production. Based on the remarkable results that I had observed first-hand in India and Pakistan, using Norman Borlaug's technology, I was a strong supporter of focused agricultural research. I argued that the United States should challenge the rest of the world: We will provide 25 percent of the financing for the growing set of international agricultural research centers if the rest of the world will provide the remaining 75 percent. The challenge was accepted and funds began to flow.

Warren Baum reported, "Fund-raising in the early years was not difficult. …The central objective of the [Consultative] Group —to reduce hunger by increasing food production in the developing countries—was universally popular …"[52]

In 1972, the budget for the four centers was about $19 million. At the beginning of the twenty-first century, the system consisted of fifteen centers and the annual expenditure was a bit over $340 million. Lowell Hardin says, "To my view this extraordinary feat in international collaboration involving over fifty donors [industrial and developing countries, foundations, international and regional organizations] would not have been possible without the wholehearted, visionary support of the World Bank and members of its talented staff."[53]

The impact of such an integrated approach was already evident in the Green Revolution. New varieties and the new technologies that make them highly productive had been the match that sparked it. In the Philippines, Ceylon, Malaysia, and West Pakistan, it was the IR8 rice, developed at IRRI. The dwarf Mexican wheat, produced by CIMMYT, provided the kindling in India and Pakistan, and it soon spread to Turkey, Afghanistan, Iran, Morocco, Tunisia, Argentina, Chile, Brazil and, a decade later, China.

Hardin wrote, "Make no mistake about it. Although I write from the perspective of a Ford Foundation person, it was the Rockefeller Foundation scientists who developed the research and training approach to problem-solving that made IRRI and CIMMYT so successful."[54] Hardin could have added that Norman Borlaug, more than any other single person, had invented the approach that made it all happen.

During my tenure as director of foreign agricultural programs in Washington, Dr. Guy Baird, a former Rockefeller Foundation scientist, was my associate director for research. His primary responsibility was to liaise with officials in the CGIAR, monitor the set of international centers, and schedule the US funding for the centers. Either Dr. Baird or I attended as observers the annual board meetings of each of the centers. In 1976, it was my lot to attend the meeting of CIMMYT's Board of Trustees. I had the distinct privilege once again of interfacing with Norman Borlaug, who was showcased at the meeting. Needless to say, the CIMMYT Board was justifiably proud of their Nobel laureate.

As of 2005, the global network consists of fifteen international agricultural research and training centers. In addition to the four mentioned above—IRRI, CIMMYT, IITA, and CIAT—the following round out the network:

• CIFOR: Center for International Forestry Research. Indonesia. Mandate: To conserve forests and improve the livelihood of people in the tropics.

• CIP: The Centro Internacional de la Papa. Peru. Mandate: Develop technology for increased production of the white, or Irish, potato.

• ICARDA: International Center for Agricultural Research in the Dry Areas. Syria. Mandate: The improvement of barley, lentil, fava bean and on-farm management of water in dry-area developing countries.

• ICRISAT: International Crop Research Institute for the Semi-Arid Tropics. India. Mandate: Improve the quantity and reliability of food production in the semi-arid tropics.

• IFPRI: International Food Policy Research Institute. Washington, DC. Mandate: Identification and assessment of issues arising from the intervention of governments and international agencies in national, regional and global food production.

• ILRI: International Livestock Research Institute. Kenya & Ethiopia. Mandate: Improve agricultural systems in which livestock are important for poor people in developing countries.

• IPGRI: International Plant Genetic Resources Institute. Rome. Mandate: Advance the conservation and use of plant genetic resources for the benefit of present and future generations.

• IWMI: International Water Management Institute. Sri Lanka. Mandate: Improve water and land resources management for food, livelihoods and nature.

• WARDA: Africa Rice Center. Ivory Coast. Mandate: Develop rice-based technologies adapted to sub-Saharan Africa.

• ICRAF: World Agroforestry Center. Kenya. Mandate: Improve human welfare by reducing poverty, improving food and nutritional security, and enhancing environmental resilience in the tropics.

• World Fish Center: Malaysia (headquarters), Bangladesh, Cambodia, Cameroon, Egypt, Malawi, Philippines, Solomon Islands. Mandate: Develop technology for productive and sustainable living aquatic resources.

The international centers were developed to supplement national agricultural research, production, and training programs, not replace them. The centers are but one link in the worldwide network of organizations attacking basic food-crop production problems on a worldwide, regional, national, and local level.

Dr. Borlaug says, "The backbone of this network is the national programs. These must be given greater financial support and staffs must be strengthened to meet the challenge of rapidly expanding food needs."

He continues, "However, the international centers are in a unique position to assist the national programs. They are independent, nonpolitical international organizations which, although originally funded by private foundations, now receive support from many diverse sources. Their scientific staffs are also international and comprise outstanding scientists representing the various scientific disciplines affecting food production."

Borlaug says, "In the early years, 1960 and 1961, it became apparent that in all of the countries that I visited—with the possible exceptions of India and Egypt—there was an extreme shortage of trained scientists. Moreover, the few scientists that were available were generally ineffective because of poor research orientation and inadequate financial and organizational support."[55]

The Mexican experience had demonstrated that one of the greatest obstacles to the improvement of agriculture in the developing countries was the scarcity of trained people. The international centers are in a unique position to contribute to practical or internship-type training in all of the scientific disciplines affecting crop and animal production.

Borlaug's early-on insistence in Mexico that his Mexican colleagues must carry out their scientific pursuits in the field—get their boots and shirts dirty—became the model for scientific training adopted by the international centers.

Borlaug training young scientists from other countries.

Chapter Ten

The Nobel Peace Prize

"I would rather take care of the stomachs of the living than the glory of the departed in the form of monuments."

—Alfred Nobel

The Nobel Prizes are the most highly regarded of international awards. The 1970 Nobel Peace Prize was awarded to Norman Ernest Borlaug, a Rockefeller Foundation field scientist, in recognition of his pivotal role in helping modernize agriculture in the developing world—providing bread for a hungry world. During the twentieth century, Norman Borlaug was the only person to have been awarded the Peace Prize for work on food production at its most basic level—on the lands of individual farmers.

When the award was announced on October 20th, Borlaug could not be reached by telephone. His wife, Margaret, took the call and then traveled thirty miles over rough and muddy roads to get to the Toluca wheat-plot nursery where he was working. At the far end of the experimental station, she found Norm and six young scientists from four developing nations, all in mud-stained

DET NORSKE STORTINGS
NOBELKOMITÉ
HAR OVERENSSTEMMENDE MED
REGLENE I DET AV
ALFRED NOBEL
DEN 27. NOVEMBER 1895 OPPRETTEDE
TESTAMENTE TILDELT
NORMAN ERNEST BORLAUG
NOBELS FREDSPRIS FOR 1970

OSLO 10. DESEMBER 1970

Certificate of Borlaug's Nobel Peace Prize.

clothes, selecting superior individual wheat plants for the next phase of experiments.

When Margaret told him that he had been awarded the Nobel Peace Prize, Norman was certain that someone was playing a trick on him. He said, "No. No. That can't be. Someone's pulling your leg." He carried on with his work. He and his young scientist associates had to select several thousand individual, superior wheat plants, thresh the grain, and get the seeds to the Sonora experimental station by November 1 for planting in the nursery.

Alfred Bernhard Nobel, born in Stockholm, Sweden on October 21, 1833, was a prolific inventor—he accumulated 355 patents—and was successful in business as well. He took a keen interest in social questions and traveled extensively in Europe and the Americas.

Nobel died at his home in San Remo, Italy on December 10, 1896. He left the bulk of his considerable estate to a fund, the interest on which was to be awarded annually to the persons whose work had been of the greatest benefit to mankind. The Nobel Foundation was established in 1900 to manage the fund.

The first Nobel Peace Prize, bestowed jointly on two Europeans, was awarded on the anniversary of Alfred Nobel's death, December 10, 1901. By tradition, all subsequent Nobel awards have been on December 10 at 10:00 a.m., the hour of Nobel's death.

The Peace Prize is administered and awarded in Oslo, Norway. All the other Nobel Prizes are administered and awarded in Stockholm, Sweden.

The Nobel Peace Prize is awarded by a committee of five, appointed by the Storting (the Norwegian Parliament) but not formally responsible to the Storting, in accordance with Alfred Nobel's will. Nobel had never told anybody why he gave the Norwegian Storting rather than a Swedish body the task of awarding the Peace Prize. What made the cosmopolitan Swede, in 1895, decide to give the task of selecting the peace prize committee to the Norwegian Parliament? Though there has been much speculation, it remains a mystery.

The Norwegian Nobel Institute was established in 1904 to assist the Nobel Committee in the task of selecting the recipient of the Nobel Peace Prize and to organize the annual Nobel events in Oslo. A consortium of professional advisers, consisting of four permanent members plus consultants specially called upon for their knowledge of specific candidates, prepares for the committee, from a lengthy annual list of nominees, a short list of those whom it finds most suitable. The advisors do not directly evaluate nominations or provide recommendations; that is the committee's responsibility.

Observing the rules given in the statutes of the Nobel Foundation, the committee does not publish the names of candidates, and nominators are strongly urged not to publish their proposals. Deliberations about the committee's choice are strictly guarded until the last moment. Each year, usually on a Friday in mid-October in the Norwegian Nobel Institute building in central Oslo, the announcement of the laureate's name is made to the press.

The announcement that Norman Ernest Borlaug had been awarded the Peace Prize was made on October 20, 1970, a day that marked the end of Norm's intense, self-directed work in wheat fields. During the remainder of that day, still wearing his boots and baseball cap, Norm faced newsmen and television crews and gave impromptu interviews. While this was going on, Margaret and the other wives of the CIMMYT staff organized a party. Norm says, "It was nearly three o'clock in the morning when Margaret and I climbed into bed, completely exhausted. Before I dozed off, Margaret told me that both Jeanie and Bill had called. And so had Stak."

Much later, in discussing the excitement of that day, Margaret said, "I had been lonely, and at times it had been difficult, but the ultimate in recognition of Norman's accomplishments had made it all worthwhile—and *very* exciting."

For the next several days, even when he went to the back corners of the Toluca experimental station to carry on his work, the press corps managed to find Norm and solicit interviews. The announcement turned Borlaug from a behind-the-scenes worker into a very public person.

Cartoon in Mexico's press symbolizing Borlaug's Peace Prize (dove), population growth (stork), and hunger (vulture).

George Harrar congratulates Borlaug.

The staff at CIMMYT headquarters was busy with telegrams, phone calls, letters and requests for television interviews with Dr. Borlaug. Some of the letters, such as ones from prime ministers and presidents, including Prime Minister Indira Ghandi of India and President Ayub Khan of Pakistan, required immediate response. A cable from President Nixon lauded Dr. Borlaug for giving Americans reason to be proud. Letters of congratulation from Henry Ford and the Rockefeller family were dear to Borlaug's heart.

George Harrar, who was now president of the Rockefeller Foundation, called to congratulate Norm: for the award of the Peace Prize, and for having stood his ground when the two had differences while they worked together in Mexico. Norm's eyes welled as he said, "Thank you, Dutch, that means more to me than you will ever know."

When the news reached Borlaug's daughter Norma Jean and the reporters wanted her reaction, she said, "My dad is a very hard-working person and I am extremely pleased that recognition has been given to one who really deserves the honor. We have been very fortunate in our home life. Even though Dad was gone ten months of the year visiting experimental plots and training agriculturalists to produce better crops, Mother is a strong unselfish woman and helped him carry on his work."

When Mr. and Mrs. Henry Borlaug in the Evans Memorial Home for the elderly heard of the achievement of their son, there were tears of joy and thankfulness for what their Norm had done to help alleviate hunger among his fellow humans. Borlaug's mother simply said, "Norm was always a good boy."[56]

Norm made plans to take his entire family—Margaret, Bill and Jeanie and their spouses, and his sisters Palma and Charlotte —to Oslo for the presentation. He was saddened that the health of his parents would not permit their going. But he was heartened to learn that his good friends Roberto and Teresa Maurer had arranged to be there. They had cashed some insurance to pay the fare.

When the Borlaug family arrived in Norway, Norm was summoned to the palace for a private audience with King Olaf V. The king was especially cordial. He was interested in Norman's Norwegian heritage. The king was familiar with northeastern Iowa, especially the town of Decorah where the Norwegian-American Heritage Museum is located, just twenty miles from where Norm had grown up. He talked fondly of his visits to America, including two times during World War II when he visited Spillville, where Antonin Dvorak had composed some of his great music.

Borlaug was awarded his prize in the auditorium of the University of Oslo on December 10, 1970. The chairman of the Nobel Committee, Mrs. Aase Lionaes, presented the diploma and the medal.

In her presentation speech, Mrs. Lionaes said among the conditions laid down in the first paragraph of Alfred Nobel's will and testament was that the award of the prize shall be made to the person who, during the preceding year, "shall have conferred the greatest benefit on mankind."

She said, "This year the Nobel Committee of the Norwegian Parliament has awarded Nobel's Peace Prize to a scientist, Dr. Norman Ernest Borlaug, because, more than any other single person of this age, he has helped to provide bread for a hungry world. We have made this choice in the hope that providing bread will also give the world peace."

She stated that Borlaug "has helped to create a new food situation in the world and has turned pessimism into optimism in the dramatic race between population explosion and our production of food." She described Borlaug's approach and his accomplishments and then said, "Behind the outstanding results in the sphere of wheat research of which the dry statistics speak, we sense the presence of a dynamic, indomitable, and refreshingly unconventional research scientist.

"Dr. Borlaug is not only a man of ideals but essentially a man of action. …

"Through his scientific contribution and his tremendous talent for organization, Dr. Borlaug has introduced a dynamic factor into our assessment of the future and its potential. He has enlarged our perspective; he has given the economists, the social planners, and the politicians a few decades in which to solve their problems, to introduce the family planning, the economic equalization, the social security, and the political liberty we must have in order to ensure everybody—not least the impoverished, undernourished and malnourished masses—their daily bread and thus a peaceful future.

"And this is precisely where Dr. Borlaug has made his great contribution to peace."

Borlaug made a brief acceptance speech in which he expressed his deep appreciation for the honor and the award. He concluded with a statement that summarized his thoughts about the future of mankind:

"There can be no permanent progress in the battle against hunger until the agencies that fight for increased food production and those that fight for population control unite in a common effort. Fighting alone, they may win temporary skirmishes, but united they can win a decisive and lasting victory to provide food and other amenities of a progressive civilization for the benefit of all mankind.

"Then, indeed, Alfred Nobel's efforts to promote brotherhood between nations and their peoples will become a reality."

Later the same day, the Nobel Committee hosted a banquet to honor the laureate. In addition to King Olaf, Norm's family and the Maurers, special guests included four representatives of agricultural organizations from Sonora, Mexico.

The next day, on December 11, Dr. Borlaug delivered his Nobel lecture, "The Green Revolution, Peace, and Humanity." In his presentation, Borlaug summarized his philosophy: "If you desire peace, cultivate justice, but at the same time cultivate the fields to produce more bread; otherwise there will be no peace."

In a moving vote of thanks to Dr. Borlaug after his Nobel Prize lecture, Professor John Sanness, a member of the Nobel Committee, said:

"On behalf of the Nobel Committee of the Norwegian Storting, I have the honor and the very great personal pleasure to express to you our gratitude for your readiness to travel across the world to receive your well-deserved prize, for your vivid and stimulating lecture and for the indelible impression we have received tonight and during our few brief days of personal acquaintance of a personality of whom until these days we could catch only some glimpses from afar.

"No member of the committee will contradict me when I venture to reveal the self-evident truth that we did not award the Peace Prize to the scientist Dr. Borlaug. We awarded it to the man Dr. Borlaug, of whom the scientist is just one well-integrated part. We would not have awarded the prize to a scientist working in an ivory tower laboratory just for the unplanned and unintended benefits, however vast, which his research might have happened to offer mankind. But from the day in 1944 when you crossed the border to North Mexico you as a man have put yourself as a scientist at the disposal of suffering humanity. You have made the fight against hunger your lifelong mission, your passionate calling, to which you have devoted your brains, the brains of a first-rate scientist, your hands, the hands of the Iowa farmer, and your open, broad, warm heart. ...

"Our sincere thanks, Dr. Borlaug, and good luck to you, to all men in your international teams and to the millions of human beings you have taken to your heart, to the leaders and the masses of the Green Revolution, racing against time."

After the ceremonies in Oslo, Norman and Margaret drove upcountry to visit the homeland of his ancestors. Norm says, "We were treated like royalty. Every moment during those few days was filled with smorgasbord, bells ringing, and children singing. The Christmas spirit was everywhere."

Meanwhile, back in Cresco, Iowa, the town fathers had designated December 20 as Norman Borlaug Day. A few months after Norman and Margaret returned from Norway, Iowa's Governor Robert Ray presented him with Iowa's Outstanding Service Award. Norm's father was not well enough to come, but his mother was there in her wheelchair. Dave Bartelma was there. Perhaps the most proud man of all, at Norm's side, was Professor E. C. Stakman, who said to Norm, "One of the things I admire about you is that your collar size and your hat size haven't changed. You are the same humble, dedicated person whom I knew as a student at the university."

Reflecting on it years later, Norm said, "The Nobel Prize hit me like a typhoon."

While he adjusted admirably to the notoriety, he often says, "I sometimes think fondly of that summer of complete isolation on Cold Mountain."

Chapter Eleven

Launching the World Food Prize

"To inspire and recognize exceptional achievement in assuring adequate food and nutrition for all."

—The World Food Prize Foundation

Among the categories of Nobel Prizes, there is no award for food production or agricultural advancements. Dr. Borlaug's honor was based on fulfillment of conditions required for recipients of the Nobel Peace Prize: The award of the prize shall be made to the person who during the preceding year shall have contributed the greatest benefit to humankind.

A dozen years after he had been awarded the Peace Prize, Borlaug petitioned the Board of Governors of the Nobel Foundation to add a category for excellence in agriculture and food. The response was, "The Nobel Foundation is well aware of the need for recognition of the importance of agriculture and food, but that since a prize for agriculture and/or food was not provided for in Alfred B. Nobel's will and endowment, it is not legally possible to establish a new prize with the use of these endowed funds."

In his deep-seated belief in its importance, Borlaug decided to try, somehow, to establish a world food prize. He says, "For the next three years I searched ineffectively for a sponsor for such a prize." Norm's long-time friend and colleague, Robert Havener, joined with him in the search. They approached the management of General Foods Corporation, who, in 1986, with the strong support of Vice President A. S. Clausi, agreed to fund a World Food Prize with a monetary value equivalent to that of a Nobel Prize at the time. Subsequently, the parent company of General Foods, Philip Morris, acquired Kraft Foods. In 1990, the chairman of the new Kraft General Foods terminated support, although Philip Morris provided half of the support for that year's prize.

For a time, it appeared that Borlaug's dream was about to evaporate. Then Clausi and Borlaug met with John Ruan, a self-made multimillionaire who, like Norman himself, had been born in a small Iowa town in 1914. In 1932, during the worst of the Great Depression, when John Ruan was a university freshman, his father died. John was forced to drop out of college and find a job. In a classic American success story, he turned a one-truck gravel hauling operation into a trucking empire with more than twenty thousand vehicles.

Borlaug met with Ruan and they quickly struck up a friendship. Norm shared with Ruan his ambition to establish a world food prize to recognize those who had made outstanding contributions to providing food and nutrition for the world's hungry. Ruan had similar objectives and graciously accepted sponsorship of the World Food Prize.

Ruan appointed Herman Kilpper, who had been president of the Ruan-owned Bankers Trust of Iowa, to manage the prize. Kilpper added a symposium, and then initiated a World Food Prize Youth Institute to reach out to high school students.

The Ruan family created the World Food Prize Foundation as the managing entity for the prize, made a $10 million endowment to the new institution and, on January 1, 2000, appointed retired ambassador Kenneth M. Quinn, a native of Iowa, as its president. The foundation recently acquired the vacated Des Moines public library building, an early 20th century edifice, as its headquarters. The Ruan family gave $5 million to rehabilitate the charming structure.

Ambassador Quinn is often asked, "What exactly is the World Food Prize?" He says he usually responds to such inquiries by quoting the President of the Federal Republic of Germany, Dr. Johannes Rau, who called the award "the Nobel Prize for Food and Agriculture."

But the longer answer, according to Quinn, is that the World Food Prize is a $250,000 annual award presented each October in Des Moines, Iowa, to inspire and recognize exceptional breakthrough achievements in increasing the quantity, quality, or availability of food around the globe. Since its inception, World Food Prize laureates have come from Bangladesh, China, Cuba, Denmark, India, Mexico, Sierra Leone, Switzerland, the United Kingdom, the United States, and the United Nations.

On or near United Nations World Food Day, October 16 each year, a World Food Prize celebration is held in Des Moines; it consists of the World Food Prize International Symposium, the Laureate Ceremony and the Global Youth Institute. Ambassador Quinn says, "Even at 91 years of age, Norman Borlaug is at the center of all three events, creating what is arguably one of the most significant celebrations of United Nations World Food Day anywhere around the world."

The World Food Prize International Symposium draws more than five hundred participants to Des Moines each year from more than forty countries and across the United States. Each year, the Symposium has a new theme. In 2004, it was the Year of Rice: from Asia to Africa. The theme was given even greater impetus by the announcement on March 29, 2004, at a ceremony hosted by Secretary of State Colin Powell at the State Department in Washington, where the 2004 laureates were announced, that the win-

Borlaug speaks at the World Food Prize Symposium.

ners of that year's World Food Prize were two exceptional scientists and rice breeders: Professor Yuan Longping of China and Dr. Monty Jones of Sierra Leone.

Professor Longping's scientific breakthrough led to the world's first successful and widely grown hybrid rice varieties, revolutionizing rice cultivation in China and tripling production over a generation. His approach to rice breeding then spread internationally throughout Asia and to Africa and the Americas, providing sustenance for tens of millions and leading to his becoming known as the "Father of Hybrid Rice."

Dr. Jones led a pioneering effort to develop new rice for Africa. In an unprecedented achievement, he recaptured the genetic capability of ancient African rices by combining African and Asian species, dramatically increasing yields, offering hope to millions of poor farmers and potentially providing a catalyst for agricultural transformation in West Africa.

Longping and Jones received equal shares of the prize at a ceremony in the Iowa State Capitol Building in Des Moines on October 14, 2004.

Ambassador Quinn says, "It was a most stirring moment when, at the conclusion of the March 29 ceremony at the U.S. State Department, Secretary Powell led the diplomatic corps in singing 'Happy Birthday' to Dr. Borlaug while a cake with 90 candles ablaze was brought forward for him."

The 2005 World Food Prize was awarded to Indian Scientist Dr. Modadugu Gupta for his pioneering work in the development and spread of aquaculture (fish farming) in Asia. Borlaug says, "This is the first time the prize has recognized aquaculture, which now accounts for more than 20 percent of the world fish 'catch.' In the future, I expect that aquaculture will play a much bigger role in the world's food supply."

The World Food Prize was created to be the highest individual honor for truly exceptional and unique achievements in improving the quantity, quality, and availability of the world's food supply, as well as the access of all human beings to it.

The first annual World Food Prize was awarded in 1987 to Dr. M. S. Swaminathan, a citizen of India, for his outstanding contributions to expanding production and availability of food throughout the world. As we have seen, Dr. Swaminathan was one of Borlaug's key collaborators in India during the early stages of the Green Revolution in South Asia. Among his many distinguished positions and accomplishments, Swaminathan served as Director of the Indian Council of Agriculture, then as Director General of the International Rice Research Institute in the Philippines from 1982 to 1988.

Dr. Robert F. Chandler, the 1988 laureate, from the United States, was founding director of the International Rice Research

Institute, where his leadership helped spur an international network of agricultural research.

Dr. Verghese Kurien of India was the 1989 recipient of the prize. He transformed the milksheds of India into cooperatives that produce, process, and market milk in the urban centers.

Dr. John S. Niederhauser of the United States was awarded the prize in 1990 for his discovery of durable resistance to late-blight disease of the potato, which boosted the food supply of many nations.

Dr. Nevin S. Scrimshaw, United States, the 1991 laureate, developed the principle of low-cost, protein-rich food products to combat malnutrition in developing countries.

Dr. Edward F. Knipling and Dr. Raymond C. Bushland, a team of entomologists, were joint laureates in 1992 for the development of the sterile insect technique to control insect parasites threatening the world's food supply.

He Kang, former Minister of Agriculture in the People's Republic of China, was awarded the prize in 1993 for spearheading large increases in agricultural output in the early 1980s, making China self-sufficient in basic food for the first time in modern history.

Dr. Muhammad Yunus, founder of the Grameen Bank in Bangladesh, was the 1994 laureate. He created innovative small, micro-credit loan programs for the poor, providing millions of people access to more food and better nutrition.

Dr. Hans R. Herren of Switzerland, who was awarded the prize in 1995, devised and implemented the biological control project for the cassava mealybug, which had nearly destroyed the entire African cassava crop.

In 1996, Dr. Henry Beachell of the United States and Dr. Gurdev Khush of India were jointly awarded the prize; they share credit for their revolutionary work to greatly improve the yield potential of rice. The rice genetic lines and varieties developed under their direction more than doubled the world's rice production over the prior three decades.

Dr. Perry L. Adkisson and Dr. Ray F. Smith were joint recipients of the prize in 1997 for their concept of Integrated Pest Management (IPM), which employs various techniques to protect crops from insect damage in an environmentally sustainable manner.

B. R. Barwale of India, the 1998 prize winner, led the way in the expansion of the private seed industry in India, which strengthened the overall seed supply and dramatically increased the distribution of high-yielding, high-quality varieties of hybrid seeds in the country.

Dr. Walter Plowright of England, 1999 laureate, was recognized for his development of a vaccine that resulted in the control of rinderpest, or cattle plague, a menace dating back sixteen centuries, from most regions of the developing world.

Dr. Evangelina Villegas of Mexico, a cereal chemist, and Dr. Surinder K. Vasal of India, a plant geneticist, shared the 2000 prize for creating a maize containing twice as much usable protein as normal maize.

Dr. Per Pinstrup-Andersen of Denmark, who at the time was Director General of the International Food Policy Research Institute, was awarded the 2001 World Food Prize for his contribution to agricultural research, food policy and uplifting the status of the poor and starving citizens of the world.

Cuban-born Dr. Pedro Sanchez received the prize in 2002 for pioneering ways to restore fertility to the poorest and most degraded soils in Latin America and Africa and offering hope to all those struggling to survive on marginal lands around the world.

Prizewinner Catherine Bertini of the United States, Executive Director of the United Nations World Food Programme, was recognized in 2003 for her leadership of the WFP in saving millions from famine and starvation.

As noted above, the 2004 laureates were rice breeders Yuan Longping of China and Monty Jones of Sierra Leone.

Dr. Modadugu Gupta of India, the 2005 laureate, pioneered the development and dissemination of low-cost techniques for freshwater fish farming in rural areas—from Bangladesh to the Mekong Basin countries—that brought a "Blue Revolution" to Southeast Asia and beyond.

The World Food Prize selection process is governed by the Board of Directors of the World Food Prize Foundation, which in turn is guided by a council of advisors in the establishment of criteria for awarding the prize and in the approval of the recommendations received from the selection committee.

The selection committee consists of nine distinguished individuals from around the world who are specialists in various aspects of food production, processing, distribution, marketing, and nutrition. Their experience covers the fields of research, policy development, and business management. Members of the selection committee remain anonymous except for the non-voting chairman, the position held by Norman Borlaug.

As of 2005, members of the Council of Advisors for the World Food Prize included:

- Norman E. Borlaug
- The Honorable George H. W. Bush
- The Honorable Jimmy Carter
- Gordon Conway, President Emeritus, Rockefeller Foundation
- A. S. Clausi, Past President, Institute of Food Technologies; Senior Vice President (Ret.), General Foods Corporation
- Senator Elizabeth Dole
- Michael G. Gartner, Past President, NBC News
- Gregory Geoffroy, President, Iowa State University
- Corazon C. Aquino, Former President, The Philippines
- M. Peter McPherson, Past President, Michigan State University
- Cynthia H. Milligan, Dean, Business Administration, University of Nebraska

- Robert S. McNamara, Former President, The World Bank
- Jonathan F. Taylor, University of London

Dr. Borlaug is justifiably proud of the Youth Institute, established in 1994. He says, "My original concept for the World Food Prize was for it to serve as a stimulus for young people to take an interest in food and population issues and go into related sciences. I think it does serve that purpose. But I am especially pleased that the Youth Institute's competition in essays on the world food situation has grown to be, perhaps, an even greater stimulus."

High school students are invited to submit research papers to the World Food Prize Foundation. From these submissions, a select number of individuals and their faculty advisors are invited to attend the Youth Institute.

The Youth Institute experience was originally offered to high school students in Iowa. It was later broadened to include other states and, in select cases, other countries. The institute increases awareness among today's youth about worldwide food supply and food security for the twenty-first century. A purpose is to encourage dedicated young adults to consider careers in food, agriculture, and natural resource disciplines.

Borlaug says, "The day after the presentation of the World Food Prize, students participating in the Youth Institute each have fifteen minutes to make presentations—they are most impressive. These are the peer groups who in fifteen to twenty years will be running things."

One of the significant benefits of a student's participation in the Youth Institute in October is eligibility to be considered for an eight-week all-expense-paid World Food Prize International Internship at a research center in Africa, Asia, or Latin America. In the summer of 2005, thirteen high school students were Borlaug-Ruan International Interns. One each went to CIMMYT in

Mexico; the International Rice Research Institute in the Philippines; China Agricultural University in Beijing; The World Fish Center in Malaysia; the Monteverde Institute in Costa Rica; Peking University in China; the International Potato Center in Peru; the M.S. Swaminathan Research Foundation in Madras, India; the International Centre of Insect Physiology and Ecology in Kenya; the Chinese Academy of Agricultural Sciences in Beijing; the International Livestock Research Institute in Ethiopia; the Brazilian Corporation of Agricultural Research in Londrina, Brazil; and the China National Hybrid Rice Research and Development Center in Hunan.

Leading educators describe this intern program as "the single most prestigious program offered to high school students." The Youth Institute is reaching students in more than 200 high schools and is expanding rapidly.

During the past decade, a remarkable number of young people have participated in both the World Food Prize Youth Institute and the eight-week Borlaug-Ruan summer intern program. Bor-

Leon Hesser, the author, and Stephanie Verenga, a 2005 World Food Prize Youth Institute participant.

laug says, "The growth in maturity and self-confidence that I have seen in the summer interns warms my heart. Many have gone on to some of the best universities in America, and usually with substantial scholarships. These are our future leaders. Many of them will become scientists." Then, with a sparkle in his eye, he says, "And some will go into international agriculture work."

Chapter Twelve

Borlaug in China

"Borlaug's humanitarian pursuits continued in the 1970s in China, where he helped increase wheat production by millions of tons a year."
—US National Academy of Sciences

On February 21, 1972, President Richard M. Nixon stepped down from Air Force One in Beijing and offered his hand to Premier Chou En-lai, to consummate one of the most historic encounters in diplomatic history. As Nixon's National Security Advisor, Henry Kissinger had managed the secret meeting that broke two decades of diplomatic silence between the United States and the People's Republic of China.

Given that dramatic breakthrough, President Jimmy Carter was able to establish official diplomatic relations between the two countries in 1978.

In 2003, at his Presidential Library at Texas A&M University, former President George H. W. Bush hosted a celebration of the twenty-fifth anniversary of the official opening of diplomatic relations with China. Chinese and American scientists participated in the two-day conference. Among other notables, Henry Kissinger was prominent.

In 1974, just two years after President Nixon's meeting with Premier Chou En-lai and Party Chairman Mao Tse-tung, Norman Borlaug was among a group of ten American agricultural scientists who spent a month on an exchange visit in China. The group, sponsored by the US National Academy of Sciences, was led by Sterling Wortman of the Rockefeller Foundation. A group of Chinese agricultural scientists visited the USA a year later.

When the Americans got off the plane, about a dozen Chinese were waiting to greet them. Through the glass barrier between Immigration and the reception area, Borlaug recognized one of the Chinese, Lou Chen Hou, who had been a fellow graduate student at the University of Minnesota; he had earned a Ph.D. in plant physiology in 1939. They had become well acquainted when they participated in Professor Stakman's seminars in 1938 and 1939. The two had not seen each other since Lou Chen graduated. Lou Chen Hou was now one of China's top agricultural scientists—a plant physiologist—and had survived the Cultural Revolution.

From the expression on Lou Chen's face, Norm knew that he had recognized him as well. It happened that Borlaug was the only one of the visiting group who knew personally any of the Chinese greeters. Norm says, "This posed a question. Should I greet him with open arms as an old friend, or would it be best from a diplomatic standpoint to be nonchalant and simply greet him in the same manner as all the others?"

This was in the waning years of the Cultural Revolution, the universities were still closed, and scientists in the experiment stations would probably be fearful of befriending the Americans. Norm decided, in view of the then-existing cool official relationship between the United States and China, that it would be best not to make a show of their personal relationship. So, when the visitors went through the receiving line to greet the Chinese, Norm simply winked with one eye when he greeted Lou Chen, and Lou Chen gave a one-eye wink in return.

The international team of scientists visited twenty agricultural research centers and seven communes, including their component production brigades. The team traveled five thousand kilometers, mostly by railroad or air. Local transport to the agricultural experiment stations was in army vehicles. Security was tight, food was rationed, and dress for all was drab army green. Through comprehensive national efforts, China had an extensive and more effective program of increasing yields and production on collective farms than did the Soviet Union. There was no starvation, though there had been massive famines during the early days of collectivization and the Cultural Revolution.

In 1977, two exchanges, one involving specialists in wheat and the other in maize, occurred between the Chinese Academy of Agricultural Science and CIMMYT scientists. Dr. Borlaug served as leader of the wheat group.

In 1979, Borlaug made a third trip to China, this time as leader of a group of four scientists and administrators from CIMMYT, including Haldore Hanson, Glenn Anderson and Eugene Saari. By this time, Norm was convinced of the great success of the Chinese agricultural program, contrasted with that of the Soviet Union, where he had visited in 1970.

Norm says, "I noticed a remarkable difference between the USSR and China in scientific pursuits. The USSR had held its scientists down under Lysenko, a 'barefoot scientist' of minimal training who decried academic scientists and geneticists. After Stalin placed him in charge of the Academy of Agricultural Sciences of the Soviet Union, Lysenko caused the expulsion, imprisonment, even death, of hundreds of scientists—including N. I. Vavilov, the USSR's most famous agricultural scientist—and sparked the demise of genetics throughout the Soviet Union. Lysenkoism lingered on for years after Khrushchev's death in 1965 and Lysenko's subsequent dismissal. The negative effect on their agriculture was apparent everywhere."

China also was slightly touched by Lysenkoism. But following the Cultural Revolution, China became much more open. Norm volunteered this anecdote to illustrate the difference between the Soviet and the Chinese approaches to agricultural science by the late 1970s and early 1980s: "When their young scientists came to CIMMYT for training, the Soviets kept a close watch on them. Someone from the Soviet Embassy would come out about once a month to check on them. By contrast, China told us, 'They are yours. Let us know if there is a discipline or a health problem. Otherwise, they are yours.' "

Given its large population, its limited cultivated land area per person, and its low per capita income, China "is one of the remarkable achievements" of the twentieth century.[57] An explosive surge in production occurred after Deng Xio Ping came to power and restored personal economic incentives by modifying the collectives and allowing free markets to develop. With only 7 percent of the world's arable land, China feeds 22 percent of the world's population.

Dr. Borlaug's influence on the agriculture of China had started several years before his first visit in 1974. Pakistan, which had friendly relations with her at the time, had indirectly supplied China with experimental wheats. Norm said, "In the spring of 1966, West Pakistan's Secretary of Agriculture Amir Ahmed Khan showed me a box of small samples of MexiPak seed and twenty other experimental Mexican lines that he personally was transporting to China."

In 1970, based on results of tests with these experimental seeds, the People's Republic of China purchased five thousand tons of Borlaug's high-yielding Mexican wheat seed from Pakistan. The purchase sparked a revolution in spring wheat production in areas where the winters are not severe, although the largest wheat area in China at that time was sown to cold-tolerant, winter-habit varieties. Later, especially during the 1990s, CIMMYT's Mexican wheats were widely grown during the summer season in north and northwest China.

From the late 1960s through the 1980s, impressive increases in yield and production of cereals occurred not only in India and Pakistan, but in the Philippines, South Korea, Taiwan, Israel, Indonesia, Turkey, Syria, Egypt, Chile, Bolivia, Argentina, Brazil, Paraguay, Uruguay, Spain, Portugal, and Italy. However, the most impressive increases in yield and production of cereals—wheat, rice, maize and millet—were in the People's Republic of China. Norm says, "Much of the increase in China was based on practices developed largely in China: varietal improvement and improved crop management practices, including use of chemical fertilizer and weed control. Production was stimulated by economic polices that encouraged adoption of high-yield technology."

China became a donor member of the CGIAR in 1983. Even before that, she had begun to work with several of the international agricultural research centers and had particularly close relations with IRRI and CIMMYT. In the drive for self-sufficiency in food, China has made particularly strong advances in the production of rice, wheat and maize. Nevertheless, production has barely kept pace with increasing population. Additional production will have to be achieved without an increase in the area devoted to crops, because land reclaimed and brought under new irrigation will be offset by land converted to other uses.[58]

At the National Press Club in Washington, DC, on October 14, 1993, Norman Borlaug announced that the 1993 World Food Prize was designated for Dr. He Kang of The People's Republic of China for the multi-pivotal role he played as a scientist, policy-maker, and cabinet minister in revolutionizing Chinese agriculture. Dr. Borlaug said:

> America has been blessed with good soil, a temperate climate, hard-working farmers and visionary leaders who launched timely and effective programs in agricultural education, research and extension. Through their collective efforts, the vast potential for production of food in America has become a reality. The result, for most of our history, has been cheap food and plenty of it. We don't think much about food because we have so much of it. But we should. There is no more essential commodity than food. Without food, people perish, social and political organizations disintegrate, and civilizations collapse. That is why it is so important and fitting that we recognize individuals who have made outstanding contributions to the quality, quantity, and availability of food in the world. By doing so, we hope to challenge some of the most talented young women and men to dedicate their lives to some aspect of the food problem.
>
> He Kang is such a man. Under his leadership, China has made extraordinary advances in the production and distribution of basic foods. No nation has made greater progress.
>
> These agricultural gains have resulted from both technological advances and governmental policy reforms. For example, the construction of a dozen new, large, modern ammonia plants and urea converters has provided Chinese farmers with access to a steady supply of nitrogenous fertilizer that has helped to greatly increase yields. For forty centuries, Chinese farmers were famous for their efficient use of animal manure, crop residues, and nightsoil; today China is also the largest producer and consumer of chemical nitrogen fertilizer in the world.

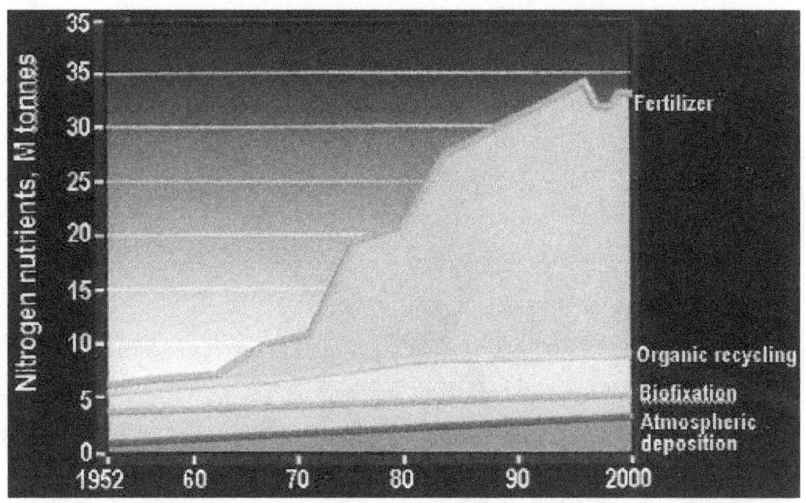

Use of organic recycling and chemical nitrogen fertilizer in China.

These technological changes were accompanied by policy changes, implemented and administered by He Kang, that effectively modified China's agricultural communes and replaced them with a family unit structure backed by a market-oriented system of 'production responsibility.' The result has not only been greater crop yields but a significant improvement in farmers' incomes and a dramatic decrease in rural poverty.

In 1995, Borlaug and Chris Dowswell reported, "The most impressive increase in cereal yield and production over the past 15 years… has been in the People's Republic of China. In 1961, the average yield and production of all cereals in that country was 1.4 metric tons per hectare and 147 million tons, respectively. By 1980, it had approximately doubled to 2.8 tons per hectare with a production of 285 million tons."[59] By 1990, yields and production had grown to 4.2 metric tons per hectare and 389 million total tons.

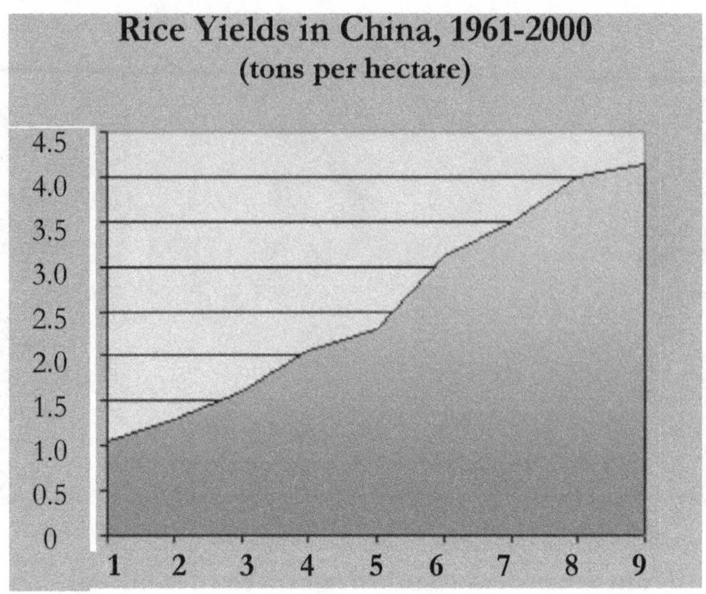

Borlaug wrote, "Impressive savings in land use have also accrued in China…through the application of modern technologies to raise crop yields. Had the cereal yields of 1961 still prevailed in 1992, China would have needed to increase its cultivated cereal area by more than three-fold… Clearly such a surplus of agricultural land is not available."[60]

Land spared worldwide with seed-fertilizer technology.

Borlaug noted at a talk in Taipei, Taiwan in 1995: "Since 1980 The People's Republic of China has been the greatest success story. Home to one-fifth of the world's people, China today is the world's biggest food producer. With every passing year, its average cereal crop yield approaches more closely that of the United States. …

"One of the driving factors in the spectacular Chinese progress in increasing yields and production has been… government policies that liberalized crop production and grain marketing systems, essentially doing away with the commune."[61]

The China National Hybrid Rice Research and Development Center, with Yuan Longping serving as director-general, was created in the early 1970s to help China become self-sufficient in rice production. As noted in the previous chapter, Professor Yuan is credited with having pioneered a breakthrough that led to the development of hybrid rice. In the three decades following the discovery, hybrid rice was planted on about half of China's rice area, resulting in a 20 percent higher yield. He was co-recipient of the 2004 World Food Prize.

Professor Yuan believes that further generation of new rice hybrids and varieties must rely on biotechnology, and that further innovations in biotechnology will be needed if China's farmers are to continue progressing toward the goal of feeding the country's growing population.

With China's population now estimated at 1.3 billion and growing, efforts to increase food production will continue to be a priority. During Dr. Borlaug's more than 15 trips to China, he encouraged them to pursue biotechnology as a most promising path to maintaining self-sufficiency in food. Norm says, "When I was in China in 2004, I gave the Nobel Guest Lecture in the Great Hall of the People to 1,500 young scientists and students from the Ministry of Science and Technology. And among other ideas, I pushed China to release a biotech rice variety to help speed the breakdown of biotechnology resistance in Europe."

Chapter Thirteen

Norman Borlaug and Jimmy Carter Join Hands for Africa

"The African continent is the main place where food production has not kept pace with population growth: its potential for a Malthusian catastrophe is great."

—Gregg Easterbrook

For nearly 20 years, Norman Borlaug has been working with farmers in Africa, alongside former President Jimmy Carter and the Nippon Foundation of Japan, in a program called Sasakawa-Global 2000.

Agricultural economist Robert Herdt, a retired vice president of the Rockefeller Foundation, says, "In the mid-1980s Norman was settling into the role of senior statesman to the world food community. The crisis spots of the 1960s were enjoying an abundance of food the pundits had never imagined. Indonesia, Pakistan, India, and China were all producing food in abundance. They no longer could be held hostage to other countries more fortunately endowed with productive capacity."[62]

But a new challenge entered the food scene.

Farmers in most of sub-Saharan Africa, even using primitive farming methods, had ample food supplies when colonialism ended in the 1960s. In fact, some countries even exported grain. With relatively small populations and vast land areas, the leaders of Africa's newly independent nations at the time saw no reason to think they would soon face widespread hunger or starvation. That thinking began to change in the 1970s, as high population growth rates outpaced increases in food production. By the 1980s, country after country began experiencing food shortages. In 1983-84, severe droughts in the horn of Africa led to a million deaths from famine in Ethiopia and Sudan.

The late Ryoichi Sasakawa, chairman of the Japan Shipbuilding Industry Foundation[63], took up the cause. Aware of the role that the high-yielding wheat and rice varieties had played in averting widespread famine in Asia during the 1960s and 1970s, he engaged Borlaug in a dialog about agriculture in Africa.

"Why has there been no Green Revolution in sub-Saharan Africa?" he asked.

Norm replied that he had little knowledge of Africa, having concentrated his efforts in Asia and Latin America. Besides, he said, "I'm semi-retired and too old to start learning now."

The next day, Sasakawa came back with "I'm 13 years older than you are, Dr. Borlaug. We should have started sooner and didn't, so let's start tomorrow!"

With that, Borlaug organized a workshop in Geneva, Switzerland, to discuss the African food problem. Former President Jimmy Carter, who had come to know Sasakawa and his philanthropy, agreed to participate.

Borlaug invited some of the architects of Asia's Green Revolution. In total, about fifty experts attended the meeting, many with extensive experience in Africa. Discussions were wide-ranging and intense. A consensus emerged that much could be done in Africa to improve the conditions of smallholder farmers with technology "already on the shelf." What was needed, many suggested, was a vigorous effort to engage farmers through agricultural extension education programs, to demonstrate the high-yielding agricultural packages that researchers could put together.

Borlaug concluded from the workshop discussions that, "to a considerable extent, the food crisis in Africa is the result of the long-time neglect of agriculture by political leaders."

He articulated the challenge: "Despite the fact that 70 to 85 percent of the people in most African countries are engaged in agriculture, most governments have either given agriculture and rural development a low priority or pursued impractical, idealistic development goals. Investments in improved roads, input delivery and grain marketing systems and in agricultural research, extension, and general education have been woefully inadequate. And cheap food policies to appease the politically volatile urban dwellers have greatly distorted production incentives for farmers."

The constraints in most of Africa south of the Sahara are daunting and many. But an overarching problem is rural isolation, due to the lack of roads, transport, and electrical energy. "Lack of infrastructure is killing Africa," Borlaug asserts. To make this point, for selected countries he cites the following data on kilometers of paved roads per million people:

USA	20,987	Guinea	637
France	12,673	Ghana	494
Japan	9,102	Nigeria	230
Zimbabwe	1,586	Mozambique	141
South Africa	1,402	Tanzania	114
Brazil	1,064	Uganda	94
India	1,004	Ethiopia	66
China	803	Congo, DR	59

Source: Encyclopedia Britannica, 2002

Norm says, "Africa needs a much broader network of roads, with many just plain, gravel rural roads, but the continent also needs some surfaced main roads with efficient connections to seaports. Asphalt paving can come later for much of the rural road system. Improved basic transport systems would greatly accelerate agricultural production, break down tribal animosities, and help establish rural schools and clinics in areas where teachers and health practitioners are heretofore unwilling to venture."

In dismay, Norm asks, "How can the world justify expending 900 billion dollars on military operations and armament and only a pittance on roads and schools?

"In South Asia, the transport infrastructure for the Green Revolution was already in place," Norm explains. "The British built railroads into the Punjab, the fertile plains of the Indus river valley. They sent in their best hydraulic engineers and built dams and canals, creating the largest contiguous irrigated area in the world.

"But the colonial powers in Africa wanted gems and minerals," he says. "So the railroads were built to the mines, and little attention was paid to agriculture. The result is that Africa has the least developed infrastructure—from roads to irrigation to electrification—of any populated region in the world."

One World Bank report estimates that until 2030 Africa will not have the transport infrastructure that was available in India in 1960. This puts African farmers at a severe disadvantage, especially in developing domestic and international trade.

In addition, droughts are frequent in many of the savannah-like grasslands of Africa, some of the most suitable lands for food production. "High-yield agriculture is more risky when the water supply isn't assured," Borlaug says. The lowlands of East Africa; the Rift Valley, from Ethiopia to Malawi; the Sahelian zone stretching from West to East Africa, all experience frequent drought. At present, only 5 percent of Africa's cultivated land is under irrigation, compared with 30 to 50 percent of different regions of Asia.

In many cases, Borlaug notes, the type of irrigation best suited to Africa is small-scale. "Water resource development has to be high on the development priority list in Africa," he says.

Africa's smallholder farmers are more resource-poor than were farmers in irrigated areas of Asia before the Green Revolution. Human and animal diseases have taken, and continue to take, a heavy toll on life and they retard economic development. Malaria kills millions each year and debilitates tens of millions. Some 30 million Africans are HIV/AIDS positive.

Diseases also affect the use of draft animals for pulling plows. Because of various insect-transmitted illnesses, such as trypanosomiasis (sleeping sickness) and East Coast Fever, there is no tradition of animal traction in sub-Saharan Africa. As a result, only hoe and machete agriculture exists in most areas. Tractors and irrigation systems are scarce.

Borlaug also blames the Cold War for several lost generations of development. He says, "Sub-Saharan African countries suffered more from the Cold War than any other region. Whether a country aligned itself with the USSR or the Western allies, it spent huge sums on armaments and military rather than on roads, schools, public health, or agriculture."

On the positive side, unlike densely populated Asia with its accompanying shortage of arable land, parts of Africa still have large areas of undeveloped land that could be used for agriculture. Without major investments in infrastructure, research, education and health, though, the land's productive capacity cannot be realized. "You can't eat potential," Borlaug muses. "You have to have a reality that allows for this potential to be realized. Sadly, too few African leaders have been willing to go all out for a Green Revolution in their countries."

With the above constraints in mind, Ryoichi Sasakawa told Borlaug that his organization, the Japan Shipbuilding Industry

Foundation, was willing to fund several pilot projects in Africa if he were prepared to lead such an initiative. Borlaug agreed, assumed technical leadership, and began selecting staff.

Jimmy Carter offered his collaboration in the political-policymaking arena. A partnership, called Sasakawa-Global 2000, was formed between the Sasakawa Africa Association and the Carter Center's Global 2000 program.

In January 1986, Borlaug and Jimmy Carter visited Ghana, Sudan, Zambia and Tanzania along with Ryoichi Sasakawa and his son Yohei. Leslie Swindale, Director General of ICRISAT, joined them. Discussions with government leaders about the prospect of establishing action-oriented food-crop projects generated strong interest. The visitors agreed to start by launching agricultural development programs in Sudan and Ghana.

To staff the two programs, Borlaug turned to former Mexican collaborators Eugenio Martinez, Marco Quinones and Antonio Valencia as well as Ignacio Narvaez, who was Borlaug's representative in Pakistan during the Green Revolution days. In addition, Borlaug hired two young Africans: Marcel Galiba of Senegal, who did a Ph.D. at Texas A&M University and had studied with Borlaug; and Michael Foster of Ghana, who did his Ph.D. thesis research at CIMMYT while a student at the University of Reading.

Borlaug's field staff was on the ground in early 1986 in Ghana and Sudan. Using rented vehicles and temporary office facilities, the team swung into action and quickly established several dozen field plots to evaluate the available technology. Fieldwork in Zambia followed later in 1986. The results of the first field trials were encouraging. Maize, sorghum and wheat yields were two to three times higher than national averages. Farmers lined up to join the program. In Ghana, the number of maize and sorghum field-demonstration plots increased rapidly, from 40 in 1986 to 78,000 in 1989. In Sudan, the team focused on irrigated wheat production.

Field extension workers and farmers were ecstatic about the

Sasakawa-Global 2000 demonstration programs. They liked the technology packages, especially in maize and wheat, and they appreciated the practical hands-on training in the technology. By 1989, agricultural policymakers in Ghana, Sudan and Zambia were abuzz in discussing the program. Substantial jumps in staple food harvests spawned hopes that a Green Revolution for Africa was on the horizon. Many African countries requested Sasakawa-Global 2000 to establish projects in their countries.

A fourth project, in Tanzania, was initiated in 1988, a fifth in 1989 in Benin, a sixth in Togo in 1990, a seventh in Nigeria in 1992. In total, the Sasakawa-Global 2000 partnership has mounted projects in 15 African countries (Ghana, Sudan, Zambia, Tanzania, Benin, Togo, Nigeria, Ethiopia, Eritrea, Mozambique, Uganda, Guinea, Burkina Faso, Mali, and Malawi).

Norm says, "There were considerable bits of information and materials available in African experiment stations, some of it produced with the international centers, but not enough effort was going into getting the packages of technology on farmers' fields for testing. So we decided in Sasakawa-Global 2000 to help the national extension services package the technologies and take them to farmers."

Working with and through national ministries of agriculture, especially with national agricultural extension services, Sasakawa-Global 2000 has worked with several million farmers to test new food production technologies. Yields in these farmer-managed demonstration plots have been two to three times higher than national yield levels, demonstrating the robustness of the recommended technologies.

The program provides each participating farmer with the technical backstopping and the needed inputs on credit to grow a test plot employing a simple package of improved technology: the best high-yielding variety available, moderate applications of fertilizer, and improved cultural practices.

"The high cost of fertilizer has been especially pernicious,"

Borlaug comments. Generally, fertilizer is two to three times more expensive in Africa than in other developing country regions. Small-scale farmers often lack the capital needed to purchase the recommended supplies. Output markets are also uncertain. Still, there has generally been good adoption of the new varieties and the associated production technology.

Except where it is too dry or too wet, maize (corn) is the main cereal grown in sub-Saharan Africa. Plants, including several root and tuber crops and pulses, constitute much of the diet south of the Sahara. For many rural dwellers, there is little milk, eggs or meat because of animal diseases and poverty.

"So, we in Sasakawa-Global 2000," Borlaug explains, "introduced Quality Protein Maize (QPM) as a benefit to Africans who are short on meat and milk." Corn with higher-than-normal levels of quality protein had been discovered by Purdue University scientists in 1963. Compared with the usual varieties, this corn, a natural mutant from the highlands of Peru, has twice the levels of the amino acids lysine and tryptophane, two essential proteins in the human diet. QPM has protein quality close to that of skim milk.

Under the direction of Dr. Ernest Sprague, head of CIMMYT's corn program, Dr. Surinder Vasal and Dr. Evangelina Villegas built on Purdue's discovery by breeding improved high-yielding corn varieties with high-quality protein (QPM). For that, they jointly received the World Food Prize in 2000.

In 1991, Dr. Wayne Haag of Sasakawa-Global 2000, collaborating with maize scientists at Ghana's Crops Research Institute, reviewed a large selection of CIMMYT's maize materials and selected a sub-set for further evaluation. From these elite materials, the researchers selected and improved a QPM variety that they named Obatanpa, which in the Ashanti region means "good nursing mother."

"In Ghana, babies are weaned by using a porridge based on maize," Borlaug explains. "When this mixture is made from flour of the QPM variety Obatanpa, the baby receives a significant improvement in nutrition. The value of this porridge, called Koko, is made even more palatable for babies by adding a pinch of 'Power Flour,' a barley malt, which causes the QPM porridge to liquefy so that the baby can be fed from a bottle and ingest a more appropriate amount of calories."

In Ghana, about 200,000 hectares are planted to the QPM variety, Obatanpa, and its use has spread to another half dozen countries in Africa. Ghana leads the way, followed by Uganda, Mozambique, Mali, Burkina Faso, and Malawi.

Borlaug says, "Africa desperately needs these simple, effective high-yield farming systems. Without the basics, we are likely to see tens of millions more undernourished African children by 2020—even if a whole Texas-sized area of wildlife habitat were cleared for additional cropland."

Commenting on the programs in Africa, Borlaug said, "With yields two to three times greater than those previously obtained with traditional technology, the receptivity and enthusiasm of these small-scale farmers is every bit as great as it was in India and Pakistan, when the Green Revolution was taking off 40 years ago. We are now working closely with national policymakers and international development agency officials to develop policies to strengthen technology delivery systems to sustain these productivity gains.[64]

"Africa needs a 'twin-track' anti-hunger strategy," Borlaug asserts. "One track is to get small-scale commercial agriculture moving, first among those farmers in the relatively more favored agricultural lands closest to markets. These are the farmers best suited and able to intensify production in the near term. This is what Sasakawa-Global 2000 has been promoting. Later, the more distant small-scale farmers can be incorporated, as production and marketing conditions improve.

"But," Borlaug says, "infrastructure remains the big, still-unsolved bottleneck, and especially the lack of roads, holding back the development of more efficient grain marketing systems. Besides improved markets, roads bring schools and medical service and help break down cultural and language barriers—everything begins to improve."

Borlaug's method emphasizes intensive farming on existing fields to reduce the pressure on farmers to constantly slash and burn, thus reducing the negative impact on the environment. By producing more food from less land, Borlaug argues, high-yield farming will preserve Africa's wild habitats, which are now being depleted by the slash-and-burn subsistence agriculture.

Traditionally, slash-and-burn shifting cultivation and complex cropping patterns permitted low yielding, but relatively stable, food production systems. Expanding populations and food requirements have pushed farmers onto more-marginal lands and have led to a shortening in the bush-fallow periods previously used to restore soil fertility. This is having disastrous environmental consequences.

The International Food Policy Research Institute recently projected that Africa is a "building catastrophe." African farms are currently locked in a downward spiral in which the traditional bush-fallow periods are shortened from fifteen or twenty years to as little as two or three—which means crop yields are declining, soil nutrients are depleted, and still more land must be planted every year to feed the people.[65]

In spite of these obstacles, Borlaug sees positive results in selected areas. Sasakawa-Global 2000 has widely demonstrated that food crop technologies exist that can double and triple current yield levels. Moreover, smallholder farmers are able and eager to take up these new technologies.

But critics voice concerns. Some point out that the majority of food-insecure people are in marginal lands, where the purchase of modern inputs is much more costly and risky. Thus, the emphasis should be on developing technologies that are less costly and risky to farmers who cultivate lands where crop failure is more common.

Environmentalists criticize Borlaug's high-yield dependence on the use of high levels of fertilizer—namely, inorganic fertilizers—and on occasion have effectively pressured donor countries and philanthropic organizations to back away from such programs in Africa.

Borlaug says, "There are also the nonsensical arguments centered on the use of organic versus inorganic fertilizers. It's not an either-or situation—it's not that simple. I say, use all the organic wastes possible; recycle these nutrients, by all means. But don't tell the world that the needs of African soils and farmers can be met solely with organic sources. That's just not practical. Finally, the claim that nutrients from organic sources are safer than those from inorganic needs to be settled. The plant doesn't give a hoot whether the 'nitrate ion' it 'eats' comes from a bag of manufactured fertilizer or decomposing organic matter. It makes no difference to the plant, since nitrogen is absorbed in the same form from either organic or inorganic sources."

Norm agrees with Vaclav Smil, University Distinguished Professor at the University of Manitoba, who says, "Without the 80 million tons of [nutrient] nitrogen consumed annually [from chemical fertilizer], the world could sustain [feed] no more than four billion people, two billion fewer than inhabit the Earth today."

Borlaug responds to critics by saying, "Some of the environmental lobbyists of the Western nations are the salt of the earth, but many of them are elitists. They've never experienced the physical sensation of hunger. They do their lobbying from comfortable office suites in Washington or Brussels. They have never produced a ton of food. If they lived just one month amid the misery of the developing world, as I have for 60 years, they'd be crying out for fertilizer, herbicides, irrigation canals and tractors and be outraged that fashionable elitists back home were trying to deny them these things."

The Borlaug-Carter-Sasakawa partnership has now been ongoing for 20 years. It's been a productive and influential partnership. Norm says, "Jimmy Carter is a genuine, down-to-earth person—a humanitarian. He is well received and admired in Africa. And it was Ryoichi Sasakawa's impatience, drive and financial backing that got us moving quickly, and largely unfettered with bureaucratic entanglements."

In Africa, "donor fatigue" has become endemic. Borlaug says, "The World Bank retreated from agriculture during the 1990s, partly because of the changed ideology of the bank, but also due to fear of green political pressure in Washington from the 1970s through the 1990s. The result has been an obstacle to feeding Africa."

Jimmy Carter and Norman Borlaug among friends in Africa.

Norm is hopeful that the new president of the World Bank, Paul Wolfowitz, will be able to implement his pledge to help transform Africa from a continent of despair to one of hope. Upon taking office on June 1, 2005, Wolfowitz said, "We cannot have a large part of the world with 600 million people left behind and sinking."[66] Wolfowitz recognizes that the World Bank over the past 20 years has under-invested in rural infrastructure and agriculture in Africa, and he has pledged to correct this imbalance. Debt forgiveness of heavily indebted African countries will also free up resources to invest in poverty reduction programs, and in getting the more productive economic sectors moving.

Dr. Borlaug is also heartened that world leaders concluded the G-8 economic summit at Gleneagles, Scotland, in early July 2005 by offering to double aid to Africa to $50 billion by 2010.

Meanwhile, populations in sub-Saharan Africa are growing exponentially, in spite of HIV/AIDS and malaria. Approximately one-third of the six hundred million people living today in sub-Saharan Africa are chronically undernourished. The amount of food the region produces for each person has been dropping for two decades. Grain crops yield half as much per acre as is produced on the lands of poor farmers in Asia.

Twenty of the twenty-five countries that the US monitors worldwide for possible famines are in Africa. Almost half of sub-Sahara Africa lives on less than one dollar per day.

Borlaug says, "People talk about the potential of the sub-Sahara region of Africa. Yes, the potential is there. But you can't eat potential."

Reflecting on the heady days of the Green Revolution in South Asia, Norm hungers for a bombshell breakthrough in Africa. He says, "We need to make a breakthrough in one or two countries. If we can do that, the money should start coming in. Maybe the World Bank would then put in some money."

With his fingers crossed, Borlaug says, "Ethiopia may be close to making a breakthrough—to foster the first Green Revolution in Africa. Uganda is another promising candidate."

It is striking that the white-haired man from Cresco, Iowa, is a household name in parts of Africa. An official of a local growers association in Ghana said, "He's our hero. … Every time we pray, we pray for Dr. Borlaug: 'Lord, we know he's elderly. Please extend his life.' "[67]

Dr. Borlaug among friends in Ghana.

Chapter Fourteen

Feeding 10 Billion People

"Eradicating chronic hunger is both a moral imperative and a profitable investment in the future of our planet. ... the cost to the world of hunger is vastly greater than the cost of ending it."

—George McGovern

Four times as many people inhabit the Earth today as when Norman Borlaug was born in 1914. Most are reasonably well fed, thanks in no small measure to Borlaug's innovative research and his untiring efforts to apply the results. But a crucial question exists for the twenty-first century: Can world agricultural production keep pace with a burgeoning human population?

Today, Dr. Borlaug says, "I am confident that the Earth can provide food for as many as ten billion people—six times the number who lived when I was born—if, and this is a big if, the world's societies support a steady stream of both conventional and biotechnology research and the economists and political policymakers stay attuned to the needs of rural development."

In 1998, Lowell Hardin began a presentation at a world conference in Rome with a sobering assessment about future support for research. He said that international agricultural research, which flourished in the 1970s and early 1980s, faces an uncertain future. He identified some of the apparent reasons why support for such research increased rapidly, then declined. He claimed that if the downward trend in investment in international agricultural research is not reversed, the momentum of essential research programs will be seriously disrupted.

At the conclusion of his presentation, Hardin said, "The lag between the time when the investment is made in research and the time when sustainable productivity gains are realized is relatively long. This fact gives rise to my greatest concern about the decline in research support. One cannot successfully run a research enterprise on a 'stop and go' basis."[68]

During the 1990s, assistance for agricultural development from international lenders and richer nations dropped by half. While support for international agricultural research was declining, global population continued to increase. Norman Borlaug worries about both of these trends. "Does the Green Revolution indicate that the war against hunger is won?" he asks. Then he says, "By no means. No good student of the world food situation would claim that the problem of hunger has been whipped. Most would agree that valuable time has been won, time that should be wisely used in checking the rate of population growth."

At a meeting of the CGIAR in Lucerne, Borlaug addressed the unsolved problem of poverty and hunger. He said, "Despite a more than tripling in the world food supply over a period of three decades, the Green Revolution in cereal production has not solved the problem of poverty and chronic under-nutrition afflicting hundreds of millions of people around the world."[69]

In a move to alleviate the disparity between the affluent and the poverty-stricken peoples of the world, the Secretary General of the United Nations commissioned the Millennium Project at the World Food Summit held in New York in 2000. One of its goals is the eradication of extreme poverty and hunger. Task Force 2 on Hunger, one of the Millennium Project's ten task forces, seeks to reduce the number of undernourished people by half—from 800+ million in the year 2000 to 400 million by 2015.

Norman Borlaug is justifiably proud that the two coordinators of Task Force 2 on Hunger are World Food Prize laureates. One is Dr. M. S. Swaminathan, who as a young scientist accompanied Borlaug on several of his trips throughout India in the 1960s. He was Director General of the International Rice Research Institute in the Philippines from 1982 to 1988, and was presented the first World Food Prize by Dr. Borlaug in 1987. The other is Dr. Pedro Sanchez, who has had a distinguished career in international agricultural research and served as Director General of the International Center for Research in Agroforestry in Kenya. He was awarded the World Food Prize in 2002.

In addition, Christopher Dowswell, Special Assistant to Dr. Borlaug in his role as President, Sasakawa Africa Association, serves as a member of Task Force 2 on Hunger. The thirty members of Task Force 2 are all global leaders in various aspects of food production.

The Food and Agriculture Organization of the United Nations estimates that current trends will reduce the number of hungry people from about 842 million today to about 600 million in 2015—only halfway toward the goal of 400 million proposed in the Millennium Declaration. The obvious conclusion is that greater effort is needed if the goal of reducing the number of undernourished people to 400 million by 2015 is to be met.

Table 14-1: Estimated Distribution of Undernourished People

	Million
India	214
Sub-Sahara Africa	198
China	135
Other Asia & Pacific countries	156
Latin America & Caribbean	53
Near East & North Africa	41

Source: Task Force 2 on Hunger, Executive Summary of Interim Report, *Halving Hunger by 2015: A Framework for Action*, February 1, 2004.

The interim report of Task Force 2 indicates that failure to alleviate hunger is most glaring in central, east, and southern sub-Saharan Africa where the number and proportion of hungry people are forecast to *increase* in most countries.

Among its proposals, the interim Millennium report suggests an annual investment of US $1 billion in agricultural research aimed at alleviating hunger. Jeffrey Sachs, director of the overall Millennium Project, indicates that financial requirements for international development—alleviating poverty and hunger—would be secured if developed countries met existing pledges of 0.7 percent of their Gross National Product (GNP). So far, only five countries—Denmark, Luxembourg, Netherlands, Norway and Sweden—have met or exceeded their pledges. The United States provides less than 0.2 percent of GNP as international development assistance.

Two things worry Norman Borlaug a lot at the beginning of the twenty-first century. One is the pervasive imbalance between the lives of people in the affluent nations compared with those in poor countries of the world. In his more than six decades of traveling the world, Norm has seen a lot of poverty, and he thinks those who are affluent can do much more to redress the balance.

The other is what Norm calls "the vast sums being spent in all countries, developed and developing, on armaments, including nuclear and other lethal weapons, while pitifully small sums are being spent on agricultural research and education designed to sustain and humanize life rather than to degrade and destroy it."

Borlaug states, "Funding for the fifteen centers in the CGIAR network that serve the entire Third World is less than $400 million, or about the value of 2.8 million tons of wheat. This compares with the more than $160 million cost for each of the planned one hundred eighty F-22A Raptors, the US Air Force's next generation of stealth fighter aircraft."

Scott Standley of the Center for Global Development in Washington, DC, shares Norm's concern. He writes, "An effective strategy of poverty prevention has been lacking from the US foreign policy portfolio. … Last year the US spent $400 billion on military operations—equivalent to the combined spending of the next 23 closest countries—and $16 billion on development assistance."[70]

Standley continues: "A more active policy of engaging the poor may also reap strategic benefits by helping to improve within developing countries attitudes toward the US, which have reached all-time lows. … Helping other countries grow and prosper helps the American economy."[71]

Borlaug is concerned that the CGIAR may be losing its focus. In a letter published in *Science* magazine in February 2004, he gave a brief summary of the growth and impact during the thirty-year period starting in 1971 of the CGIAR and the international research centers under its umbrella. In his forthright manner, he states, "But somehow in this evolution, the CGIAR lost touch with its original purpose—to feed the hungry. It has become an unwieldy and uncoordinated beast, with too many masters and proliferating goals."

In that same letter, he noted, "The World Bank reports that plant breeding research at CGIAR centers has declined 6.5 percent annually for the last decade." Borlaug ends his letter by challenging the World Bank to "help refocus the CGIAR mission on raising smallholder agricultural productivity…"

Even if current per capita food consumption remains constant, Borlaug estimates that population growth will require that world food production must be increased by 57 percent by 2025, as compared with 1990. Most of this increase, between 70 and 80 percent, must come from land currently under cultivation, because in densely populated South Asia and East Asia, little new land is suitable to opening for cultivation.

Ever the optimist, Borlaug outlines some of the possibilities he sees for future increases in global food production. "Fortunately, many improved agricultural production technologies already exist, or are well advanced in the research pipeline, and are only partially exploited, that can be employed in the future to raise crop yields. Large unexploited 'yield gaps' exist in virtually all low-income, food-deficit developing nations, as well as in the former Soviet Union and Eastern European countries. Yields also can be increased 50 percent or more on land now under cultivation in much of Southeast Asia and Latin America and by 100 to 200 percent in much of sub-Saharan Africa."

Among the possibilities that Borlaug sees is the agricultural potential of the newly independent states of the former Soviet Union. In the aftermath of the breakup of the Soviet Union in the early 1990s, grain output plummeted. In Ukraine, for example, which had been the breadbasket of Europe during much of the nineteenth century and was a stalwart in grain production for the Soviet Union, production fell to such a low that Ukrainians could barely feed themselves. Nonetheless, with privatization of their farms and the development, however gradual, of private agribusinesses to support farming, Ukraine could once again become a breadbasket. Other republics of the former Soviet Union, as they recover economically, may also contribute to the global availability of food grains.

Borlaug is especially excited about the tremendous developments during the past two decades for the Cerrado region of Brazil, a very large area of formerly infertile soils with toxic amounts of soluble aluminum. Borlaug was one of the first scientists to champion development of the Cerrado.

Norm says, "Within the past twenty-five years, high-yielding technologies developed by soil science, agronomy, and plant breeding research have opened the door to expanding these cultivated areas enormously. The use of dolomitic limestone plus fertilizer containing nitrogen, phosphorous, potash, sulphur, zinc, boron and molybdenum, together with high-yielding, aluminum-tolerant varieties of soybeans, corn, cotton and improved grasses, provide the potential of converting 200 million hectares [500 million acres] of acid-soil savanna—formerly non-productive and nearly worthless—into a productive agricultural area, larger in size than the entire US Corn Belt. And yields of some crops—especially soybeans, corn, cotton and improved pasture grasses—are approaching those of the US Corn Belt."

During the past 20 years, perhaps one-third of this vast acid-soil savanna in Brazil has been opened successfully by employing the new technology. Borlaug says, "It is a boom-country frontier! The Cerrado has made Brazil the second largest producer and exporter of soybeans in the world and a major corn and cotton producer and exporter as well. The production of beef cattle and dairy products also has been revolutionized by improved forage production and cattle breeds adapted to this environment."

Enthusiastically, Borlaug says, "Were I younger, I would be tempted to migrate to the booming agricultural frontier of the Brazilian Cerrado."

Gregg Easterbrook notes that the evolving prospect for the Cerrado "is an example of agricultural advances and environmental protection going hand in hand: in the past decade the deforestation rate in the Amazon rain forest has declined greatly, partly because the Cerrado now looks more attractive."[72] As a result of the breakthrough research, the cost of preparing the Cerrado for agriculture is much, much less than the cost of clearing the tropical forest.

Experience in the Cerrado of Brazil during the past two decades yields the possibility of opening lands in other parts of the world that have been thought to be non-productive.[73] Large areas with soils similar to those of the Cerrado exist in Paraguay; the lowlands of Bolivia, Peru and Colombia; and in Venezuela. Borlaug says, "Within the next three or four decades, South America is likely to replace North America—the USA and Canada combined—as the largest agricultural production area in the world."

Dr. Borlaug feels confident that the type of technology that has opened up the Cerrado is applicable to vast areas of sub-Saharan Africa, a substantial part of Indonesia, and a significant part of southeast China—lands that have been low-yielding and, until now, thought to be nearly worthless, especially in Africa, and to some extent in the other areas. Borlaug says, "But the development of these new boom-agriculture frontiers is handicapped by inadequate infrastructure: railroads, barges, highways, and roads."

Dr. Borlaug concludes that perhaps 20 to 30 percent of the future needs for food may come from increases in production from expanding the area of cultivated lands, as noted above. The stark reality is that 70 to 80 percent must come from higher yields. That will require both a continuing stream of research to develop better technologies and widespread efforts to get the improved methods adopted—commonly known as extension. To make this point, Borlaug says, "Research results do not automatically flow to farmers—active extension efforts are required."

Norm says, "Crop productivity can be increased all along the line—in tillage, water use, fertilization, weed and pest control, and harvesting." Then he adds, "But for the genetic improvement of food crops to continue at a pace sufficient to meet the needs of a growing population, both conventional breeding and new biotechnology methodologies will be needed."

Fedoroff and Brown, in the book *Mendel in the Kitchen: A Scientist's View of Genetically Modified Foods,* note that "by the end of the 20th century, increases in the yields of corn, wheat and rice had begun to decline year by year, even as Earth's population continued to grow by some 80 million people each year."[74] They indicate that the yield limits of most food plants are fast approaching, which means that science will have to find other methods to double or even triple food production to provide for the growing populations. How is this going to be possible?

Fedoroff and Brown argue that molecular approaches hold the promise of being the most environmentally conservative way to increase our food supply for generations to come while helping us to become better stewards of the Earth.[75] They say we have two alternatives: "We can cultivate more land, knowing that land put under the plow is land taken away from black bears and monarch butterflies, Bengal tigers and tropical birds. Or we can produce more food from the land that is already being farmed." The latter alternative will require a continuing stream of research, both conventional and biotechnical.

What is biotechnology, or bioengineering, or genetic modification? These terms, often used interchangeably by non-scientists, denote manipulations by scientists to transform crop plants to add traits that the plants did not possess before. With this new technology, a genetically modified plant can be produced by inserting a gene—"gene-splicing"—to create a new plant with highly specific characteristics.

Borlaug says, "For 10,000 years, farmers have been genetically modifying the makeup of the crops they grow. The early farmers selected in wild populations of plants for fast growth, larger seeds and sweeter fruits. The genetic variation in the wild population of the crop species that eventually became our crop varieties originated mostly from natural crossing or hybridization done by Mother Nature; early farmers selected the best individual plants from populations that fitted their needs. Naturally occurring mutations also contributed to genetic variations in wild populations. These processes were repeated for thousands of years.

"Then," Borlaug says, "beginning with the time of Friar Gregor Mendel's discovery of the basic laws of inheritance in the middle of the nineteenth century, man began planned-parenthood crossing, or mating between different closely related plant species, to combine the desirable traits of the two parents. This is the technique and method of plant and animal breeding that has been used to improve crops for the last 150 years, the methods that I used to produce the broadly adapted, high-yielding, disease-resistant dwarf wheats." But conventional Mendelian genetics and plant breeding—because of sterility—was limited to using only closely related plant species as parental stocks.

About thirty years ago, new biotechnological techniques made it possible to break the sterility barrier—to extract individual genes at the molecular level from taxonomically distantly related species and incorporate them into our best crop varieties. This was a great leap over traditional Mendelian genetics and plant breeding methods. It opened an entire new world of exciting possibilities.

Biotechnology, or transgenetic research, has resulted in incorporating valuable new traits into maize and cotton, for example, to control serious insect pests without the use of chemical insecticides. Similarly, genes have been incorporated into soybean varieties to facilitate weed control. Currently, research is underway to incorporate genes for resisting drought, frosts and different fungal and viral diseases into important crop species.

Borlaug says, "I dream of the possibility of using transgenetic research to transfer to wheat the immunity that rice has to all three species of rust—stem, stripe, and leaf. And, hopefully, gene combinations will be found through future transgenetic research that will increase yields higher than those achieved by plant breeding."

Borlaug says, "Compared with conventional breeding, genetic modification offers a wider choice of genes, a greater possibility of finding a gene that would produce the desired characteristic. What we're doing now is speeding up the process so we can provide food for the world's rapidly expanding population."

Transgenetically modified crops have attracted worldwide attention since newly developed "biotechnology" seeds became available during the 1990s. Proponents of this technological innovation assert that the seeds have the potential to revolutionize agriculture, even in developing countries. Critics warn that the environmental and health effects are uncertain and cultivation of genetically modified crops could have adverse effects. Seldom in agriculture have viewpoints differed so widely. Thinking rapidly polarized, on both sides of the Atlantic.

Proponents of genetic modification claim a number of benefits to society, including environmental benefits. The technology can help crop plants resist pests and diseases, improve nutritional quality, resist drought, and tolerate salt in irrigated land. In crops with built-in resistance to insect pests, the use of chemical pesticides is substantially reduced.

Regarding nutritional quality, an exciting possibility known as "golden rice" because of its amber hue has the potential to reduce malnutrition substantially in developing countries for which rice is a main staple. This strain of rice has been genetically engineered to contain a higher level of vitamin A, which reduces blindness and boosts the health of poor people in developing countries. The potential economic effects of adopting the innovation in Asia suggest the farm productivity gains could be dwarfed by the welfare gains resulting from the potential health-enhancing attributes of golden rice, which would boost the productivity of unskilled workers among Asia's poor.[76]

With developing countries in mind, scientists are designing new seeds that resist the particular pests and diseases that ravage crops in the poor tropical regions of Africa, Asia and Latin America. Biotech potatoes, for example, have been developed to resist the ravenous Colorado potato beetle. To be acceptable to farmers, the individual "transgenetic" genes must be incorporated into the best current commercial crop varieties.

Opponents of the new biotechnology express concerns about the impact of genetically modified crops on human health and the environment. Criticism of the use of genetic-manipulation technologies comes to a large extent from environmental activists such as Greenpeace, a transnational non-governmental organization, and other ecology groups. Critics claim that biotech crops would poison people, create new food allergies, and unleash "superweeds" that would overwhelm the natural environment. Greenpeace has been protesting against the new genetically modified rice.

Activists in the European Union claim that genetically modified crops are risky. Succumbing to the pressure, the European Union officially blocked imports of biotech commodities for several years. By late 2004, though, European roadblocks had started to crumble.

Borlaug says, "The motivation of some rich countries to ban food imports from countries that grow genetically modified crops could possibly be a genuine concern for food safety or the environment. Or maybe it's because it provides economic protection for their farmers."

A primary weapon of the anti-biotech activists is fear. As a case in point, European activists told African governments that American corn containing the Bt gene, donated as food aid, was poisonous. The President of Zambia personally ordered thousands of tons of American corn—the same corn we eat in our corn flakes and taco chips—deported from his country despite the food crisis.[77]

Borlaug opines that there have always been those in society who resist change. But he is puzzled at the intensity of the attacks against genetically modified crops given the potential environmental benefits that such technology can bring by reducing the use of pesticides and sustaining wildlife preserves and recreational green spaces, initiatives that the attackers generally espouse.

Partly as a response to critics, but more importantly as a prudent means of determining the risks, agricultural biotechnology has arguably been submitted to greater scrutiny than any technology ever introduced into farming. A large number of government agencies worldwide have reviewed the science and approved its use. In the United States at least three cabinet-level government agencies examine each biotech crop before it is approved for planting. And state agencies also regulate the process.

Borlaug comments on this paradox: "Activists have resisted research and governments have overregulated it."

A committee set up by the National Academy of Sciences of the United States has been studying the possible problems. A report published by the Academy in 2004 states:

"All foods, whether or not they are genetically engineered, carry potentially hazardous substances or pathogenic microbes and must be properly and prudently assessed to ensure a reasonable degree of safety. Furthermore, all crop strains, including [crops produced with organic fertilizer], potentially express traits generated by various forms of induced mutagenesis. …

"To date, no adverse health effects attributed to genetic engineering have been documented in the human population," according to the National Academy of Sciences.[78]

In the year 2000, Norman Borlaug served on a twenty-person joint US-European Union Biotechnology Consultative Forum, appointed by President Clinton and Romano Prodi, president of the European Commission. Most of the experts on the panel agreed that agricultural technology holds great promise to make dramatic and useful advances during the twenty-first century. The most prestigious national academies of science in North America and Europe also came out in support of genetic engineering to improve the quantity, quality, and availability of food supplies.

Despite criticism and bureaucratic roadblocks, adoption of genetically modified crops has proceeded rapidly in the United States. And Europe is beginning to moderate. A December 2004 news dispatch states: "Even Europe, where opposition has been stiffest, is gradually warming to the idea of genetically modified crops. This year, the European Union ended a six-year moratorium when it approved imports of two varieties of genetically modified corn sold by Monsanto and its Swiss rival, Syngenta."[79]

Borlaug states, "If low-income, food-deficit nations—which desperately need access to the benefits of science and technology—are being advised by governments and pressure groups in privileged nations to reject biotechnology, based on ideologically inspired pseudo-science, there is reason for serious concern. To attempt to deny such benefits would be unconscionable."

Some argue that organic rather than chemical fertilizers should be used to solve the world food problem. Borlaug praises China for making maximum use of organic fertilizer; at the same time, he states, China is now the largest producer, importer and consumer of ammonia/urea, a chemical nitrogenous fertilizer.

Borlaug says, "Some organic gardening enthusiasts insist that the wide use of organic fertilizer could satisfy all the fertilizer needs. I've always said there should be no debate between the use of organic or chemical fertilizers. Use all the organics available, but for God's sake, don't try to tell the world that we can produce the food that's needed without chemical fertilizers."

In his usual down-home manner, he adds, "This is nonsense. The amount of composted organic animal manure that would be needed to produce the seventy million metric tons of chemical nitrogen used today would be about 4.7 billion tons—quite a dung heap and quite an aroma—were it available. This volume of organic material is equal to twice the weight of the world cereal production and would require a three-to-four-fold increase in world animal production."[80] Borlaug says, "The extra land required to grow feed for the additional livestock needed to produce more manure would be better used to grow food for hungry people."

As indicated above, Dr. Borlaug is a firm believer in the use of genetically engineered crop varieties to help meet the world food needs. He describes biotechnology as a new tool that can help the world produce enough food to feed its growing population while reducing the pressure to convert pristine wilderness into cropland. He makes his position clear when he says, "Mother Nature has been creating transgenetic plants—crossing genetic barriers—for eons. Responsible biotechnology is not the enemy; starvation is."

Chapter Fifteen

Distinguished Professor

"There is intensity in his manner and animation in his gestures."
—Don Paarlberg

In 1979, at age 65, Norman Borlaug officially retired from the directorship of CIMMYT's international wheat program. If that sounds as if he went into retirement, think again! Norm Borlaug is not the retiring kind.

Norm had demonstrated throughout his career that he was, by nature, a teacher. When word got out that he was retiring from CIMMYT, a number of universities courted him; each would like to have him serve, however briefly, as a distinguished professor on its campus. The CIMMYT Board of Trustees also wanted him to stay on for as long as possible as a consultant, to work closely with Glenn Anderson, whom the board appointed as Norm's successor.

In 1980, Borlaug accepted an appointment as Honorary Visiting Professor at his alma mater, the University of Minnesota, to teach courses and lead seminars. Because of his background in forestry as well as in plant pathology, Weyerhaeuser, the interna-

Norman Borlaug, E.C. Stakman, and Glenn Anderson.

tional forest products company, pleaded for some of Norm's time. He agreed and spent three months with Weyerhaeuser during the time he was at the University of Minnesota. He also served periodically as a part-time consultant at CIMMYT. During Norm's time as director of the wheat program at CIMMYT, Weyerhaeuser sent several of their scientists, including their director of research, to CIMMYT to observe Borlaug's research procedures. The US Forest Service and the colleges of forestry at several US universities also sent scientists. Even though the life cycle of trees is, of course, much longer than that of wheat, the forest scientists were intrigued with Norm's processes and methods and began to adopt some of them in their forestry research.

Norm was deeply saddened in early 1981 to learn that Dr. Glenn Anderson had died. At the request of the CIMMYT Board of Trustees, Norm went back for a year to direct the wheat program.

Subsequently, in addition to serving part-time as a senior consultant at CIMMYT, he resumed a formal teaching career. From 1983 through 1985, he served one month each year at Cornell University as the Andrew D. White Distinguished Professor at Large. He enlivened the Ithaca campus with his forthright views on agriculture, the environment, and development.

At the University of Florida, Borlaug was given an honorary doctorate when he gave the inaugural York Lecture, in honor of E. T. York, retired chancellor of the Florida University system, and his wife Vam. In 2004, he also gave the E. T. and Vam York lecture at Auburn University, which is the alma mater of the Yorks.

In 1984, the University of Florida's administration tried to convince Borlaug to come to their campus as distinguished professor. They were a bit too late. Perry L. Adkisson, then deputy chancellor, and later chancellor, of Texas A&M University, had already recruited him to become their Distinguished Professor of International Agriculture.

Professor Borlaug at his desk.

Each fall semester for the last 20 years, Professor Borlaug has taken up residence at Texas A&M and continues to enliven that campus. Initially, he taught graduate courses in which he described the evolution of food and agriculture through time—how societies have organized to feed their growing populations. It was a tough course, with a reading list more characteristic of a five-credit course rather than two. Norm says, "It should have been a yearlong course, but we had to crowd it into one semester because I was committed to serve as consultant to CIMMYT, and had the Sasakawa-Global 2000 program to oversee." Borlaug offered the graduate course for 10 years. Some 150 students, from the USA and many developing countries, took it for credit; while another 50 to100 participated as observers.

Until recent years, when her eyesight dimmed, Margaret joined Norman at College Station. Together they enjoyed the campus festivities. While it is rare for Borlaug to stay in one place for very long, he tried hard not to miss class during the semester when he was teaching. He remained in College Station for most of each semester. This, too, was rare for Margaret, who had grown accustomed to his being away most of the time. Thus, it is not surprising that she enjoyed the time at College Station.

"Starting with the 1995 fall semester," Norm says, "it was decided that my graduate level course was too restrictive in the number of students I was exposed to, and not the best use of my background. Now, I'm available and give seminars and general lectures on food, population, the environment, forestry and wildlife to many different classes and student clubs. The lectures are intended for undergraduates, although some grad students and even professors sit in."

Professor E.C.A. Runge, who was chair of the department of soils and plant sciences at the time Borlaug was hired, says, "Norm is very good with students, both undergraduate and graduate. He is willing to spend time one-on-one with them. He also is very effective in giving seminars and lectures to broad interest groups of student and faculty organizations. He is most effective giving guest lectures and meeting with student organizations. It has spread his influence on campus to a much wider audience."

Dr. Runge continued, "Norm is willing to take on issues that others might duck. When fertilizer and biotech were being questioned, he just kept going like the 'Energizer bunny.' His presence enriches the discussion. He has the unique ability to make people better when he is present and part of the discussion. He has never met a stranger and he does not duck issues. He meets the challenge head-on and keeps going."

Joe Dixon, Emeritus Professor, Soil Mineralogy, said, "Although I am a soil scientist and he focused on plants, he made me and my students seem important. Dr. Borlaug is a man of convictions. He has eternal optimism that we can apply new concepts for crops and soils and feed the world in spite of the naysayers who are suspicious of new plant breeding and genetics concepts. He sets an example for all of us with his work ethic."

Professor Lloyd Rooney, a food science professor in soil & crop sciences, frequently asks Norm to speak to his students. He said, "Dr. Borlaug has presented many seminars to our food science and technology students. For many it is their first real introduction to multidisciplinary crop improvement programs and what they mean in terms of world food production and nutrition. Borlaug has a knack of grasping their full attention and getting them to think outside their own little box. He opens their eyes to real world problems and does it in a very colorful, simple style that makes an instant positive impression. He challenges the students to become scientists or politicians that make a difference, and somehow gets them to understand that 'it is not a perfect world and one cannot wait for perfection to move forward.'"

In October 1999, in recognition of their Nobel laureate's distinguished service, Texas A&M dedicated a new science building: Norman E. Borlaug Center for Southern Crop Improvement. "This is a well-equipped plant biotechnology research center,"

Borlaug notes. "The challenge is to integrate the work of the Center, which is focused on fundamental research, with the applied research disciplines in plant breeding, including pathology, entomology, agronomy, and industrial and nutritional quality."

Texas A&M University and Borlaug also work together on a number of international projects, including collaborative research in maize and wheat with CIMMYT. A new initiative is now under way, in which the university plays an important role, to expand training opportunities at other US land grant universities and US Department of Agriculture laboratories for young and upcoming agricultural professionals from developing countries.

The Borlaug International Science and Technology Fellows program was announced in March 2004, at Borlaug's 90th birthday celebration. On that occasion, Secretary of Agriculture Ann Veneman described a major new US initiative to expand training and educational assistance to promising young leaders in science and technology from the developing world, in partnership with the United States Agency for International Development (USAID).

Over his 60-year international career, Borlaug has been instrumental in helping scores of young men and women from more than sixty countries pursue graduate training in agriculture at US universities, as well as thousands to attend in-service training courses to improve their practical research skills to complement their academic studies.

"I believe fervently that practical, hands-on training is essential to the conquest of hunger and to building lasting ties between America and the people of developing nations," Borlaug says. "I am so pleased that the US government and the university community are again becoming more engaged in international agriculture, as was the case in the 1960s and 1970s."

The Borlaug International Science and Technology Fellows program was quickly set in motion after its announcement on March 28, 2004. During the first year of operation, USDA, in cooperation with USAID and several land grant universities, brought more than fifty Borlaug fellows to the United States for short-term training. Individualized programs—lasting four to six weeks—were developed for each fellow at one of a half-dozen universities and USDA research laboratories. Establishing a mentoring relationship between each Borlaug Fellow and a senior US agricultural scientist is a unique feature of these fellowships. Once the Borlaug Fellow returns home, the mentoring relationship continues with follow-up visits by the mentor to the fellow's home institution. Texas A&M University hosts about one-fourth of the Borlaug Fellows.

Because there has been considerable attrition among scientists at most national agricultural research systems over the past decade, the Borlaug Fellows program comes at a crucial time. USDA plans to increase the number of Borlaug Fellows to 100 each year and add a new component to the program—graduate study grants. The grants will go to aspiring young scientists from sub-Saharan Africa in support of their master's degree thesis research. Typically, graduate study fellows do their thesis research at one of the CGIAR international agricultural research centers in collaboration with the land grant university where the graduate degree is being pursued.

As new funding is mobilized, a third component, the Borlaug Agricultural Policy Executive Leadership Course, will be initiated in 2006 or 2007. The course will be offered to senior agricultural research managers or ministry of agriculture officials, and will focus on a range of agricultural science and trade-related issues.

Many other activities at Texas A&M University occupy Borlaug's time: international conferences, visits to Texas A&M's experiment stations, and discussions with crop commodity groups and researchers.

Borlaug is also involved with the George H.W. Bush Presidential Library and Museum as well as the Bush Policy Research Center, located on the Texas A&M campus in College Station. He lectures once each year in the policy center and attends special events at the museum.

Texas A&M's Academy of Young Leaders has become a Borlaug favorite. The Academy is made up of outstanding Texas A&M University undergraduates who compete to be selected for the program. Throughout the year, Young Leaders get to hear and discuss issues of national and global importance with Dr. Borlaug, former President Bush, and many other leaders. Norm says, "This is another excellent youth leadership and development program that often makes a difference in the paths that young people take in life. Being around these bright-eyed young people helps keep the flames alive in me, too." He adds, "I don't know who benefits the most."

Chapter Sixteen

Norman Borlaug's Legacy

"Borlaug's unique combination of technical innovation, idealism, energy, and impatience with bureaucratic inefficiency took entire countries from starvation to self-sufficiency in the space of a few years."
—"Biographical Essay," *World of Genetics*

Every schoolchild in Iowa knows about Norman Borlaug. Iowa's school curricula put him in about the same category as George Washington and Abraham Lincoln. The people of Iowa want more Americans to know about their "Hero of Hunger." A sculptured statue of Dr. Borlaug graces a prominent place in the county-seat town of Cresco, Iowa.

Norman Borlaug's boyhood home in Howard County, Iowa, which was donated by Borlaug to the Norman Borlaug Heritage Foundation, is being preserved as a living memorial to his life and values. The buildings, landscape and setting enable visitors, especially school children and other young people, personally to experience part of the history, community and environment that shaped a world leader, inspiring them to leadership as well.

The one-room schoolhouse that Norman, his father and grandfather all attended has been moved to the Borlaug farm site. Toward the end of the twentieth century, the old building was slated to be torn down. When Borlaug's sister Charlotte learned that, she called Norman to tell him. Norm's immediate response was, "Buy it!" She did. Charlotte's husband inspected the structure carefully and reported that it was still sturdy enough to withstand moving. Arrangements were made to move it intact to the Borlaug homestead, where it has been restored and opened to the public.

This community project is more than historic preservation. It illustrates the values that are exemplified throughout Norman Borlaug's life: service to humanity, scientific achievement, and reverence for nature, spirituality, and commitment to education. These values are interpreted through the natural beauty of the rural community, its country school, the nearby community church, and the Borlaug family farm.

The Norman Borlaug Heritage Foundation

The Norman Borlaug Heritage Foundation, established in July 2000 with a volunteer board and consultants, is a non-profit corporation dedicated to promoting education programs and projects which reflect the lifetime achievements and philosophy of Dr. Norman Borlaug.

The Foundation has established a program of study and outreach to bring Borlaug's remarkable scientific and humanitarian contributions to the public, especially the youth. The Foundation Board selects residency participants to research and create work in their areas of expertise while spending a portion of their stipend time, especially during the summer months, at Borlaug's boyhood farm. Resident participants, involved in both scholarly research and creative discovery, travel to schools and communities discussing issues related to Dr. Borlaug's life and work.

In an age when children lack heroes of substance to serve as role models, the Foundation recognizes that Dr. Borlaug has displayed all the characteristics of a great American hero. Through this educational residency program, students and communities are encouraged to serve humankind with the same conviction and tenacity that have guided Dr. Borlaug throughout his life.

The Foundation Board reserved five acres at the boyhood farm for the development of a Borlaug Education Outreach Center. Plans for the future, as and when funds become available, include an Interpretive Center, studio, living accommodations, small study/library, science and art exhibition hall, greenhouse, board office, board room, and rooms for public and educational activities. The Borlaug farm is being restored to its 1930s appearance, reflecting the sights, sounds and smells of Norm's farm life. The 1921 home, the barn Borlaug helped his father build in 1929, and other farm buildings are being restored. The farm will continue in pasture and cropland, with Borlaug-designed crop demonstrations, walking trails and creek bridges. A small forest preserve is planned for the future.

Buildings on the Borlaug Heritage Farm.

Borlaug Hall, University of Minnesota

Beginning in the late 1950s, Dr. Borlaug, a triple alumnus of the University of Minnesota, began receiving a stream of honors from his alma mater. Then in 1985, in recognition of his outstanding accomplishments, the trustees of the university voted to dedicate a wing of a new science building in his name. Borlaug Hall, sitting on a hill on the St. Paul campus, joins Stakman Hall, named after the university's great plant pathologist and the preeminent mentor to Norman Borlaug, and Hayes Hall, named for H. K. Hayes, Norm's professor of plant genetics.

Dr. Clive James, a Canadian citizen who was born in Wales, who was at the time deputy director general for research at CIMMYT, gave the inaugural address at the dedication of Borlaug Hall on September 20, 1985. Dr. James summarized the outstanding contributions that three distinguished University of Minnesota alumni had made in fighting world hunger: E.C. Stakman, George Harrar and Norman Borlaug. He noted that Stakman was the principal professor of both Harrar and Borlaug and that "the *troika* of Stakman, Harrar and Borlaug, all plant pathologists trained at the University of Minnesota, had had a profound effect on the international wheat research conducted in Mexico, from its very genesis."

James recalled that during Dr. Stakman's visit to Mexico in April 1977, Norm Borlaug said, "I have imagined that the difference between the teachings of Socrates in ancient Greece and those of Professor Stakman in Minnesota is one of surroundings. Socrates and his pupils walked among the olive trees, and 'Stak' and his students walked among the wheat fields looking for rust. Both teachers transcended the limits of one discipline to give their students a profound perception of humanity and its problems."

Then James said, "If Stakman is the Socrates of plant pathology in Minnesota, then only one man can be its Plato, and he is Dr. Norman Borlaug, the pragmatist and practitioner, the integrator and the implementer. Norman Borlaug's greatest contribution to the advancement of science is probably his unique ability to integrate plant pathology with all other disciplines in the quest of that elusive but ultimately most important target of all—increased wheat productivity."

In conclusion, Dr. James said, "Let the Norman Borlaug Hall that is being generously dedicated today stand as a mark of respect and honor for a distinguished alumnus, and be a constant reminder of the importance of international agricultural research and the need for interdisciplinary research in the interest of science, global security and quality of life in tomorrow's world."

On the day Borlaug Hall was dedicated, Norm reflected on E.C. Stakman's influence on his life. To a packed lecture hall Borlaug said, "Stak had a reputation for instilling commitment. That man lit the skies for me. He made me reach for things I thought were beyond my grasp."

Other Namesake Institutions

A number of other institutions around the world have dedicated buildings, centers and institutes in Dr. Borlaug's name.

In 1983, the Norman E. Borlaug Center for Farmer Training and Education was christened at Santa Cruz de la Sierra, Bolivia.

The Norman E. Borlaug Building at CIMMYT headquarters in Mexico was dedicated on September 22, 1986. Grants for the building's construction were provided by Ryoichi Sasakawa, Chairman of the Japan Shipbuilding Industry Foundation, and the government of Japan. A strategically located plaque inside the building states, "No matter how excellent the research done in one scientific discipline, its application in isolation will have little positive effect on crop production. What is needed are venturesome scientists who can work across disciplines to produce appropriate technologies and who have the courage to make their case with political leaders to bring these advances to fruition."

On May 31, 1997, Dr. Borlaug officially inaugurated the Norman Borlaug Institute for Training and Research in Plant Science, De Montfort University, Leicester, United Kingdom. The Norman Borlaug Institute is comprised of four centers of excellence in plant science: the UK Centre in Leicester; the Bulgarian Centre in Sofia; the Czech Centre in Prague and Olomouc; and the Chinese Centre in Beijing and Shanghai. Scientists of the Institute are committed to developing strains of crop plants that require low inputs of chemicals and have a low environmental impact, and that give high yields of quality produce. Scientists benefit from the Institute's International Advisory Board, whose members are based at other institutions worldwide.

In October 1999, the Southern Crop Improvement complex at Texas A&M University was dedicated and named the Norman E. Borlaug Center for Southern Crop Improvement, in recogni-

Professor Borlaug at the Norman E. Borlaug Center for Southern Crop Improvement, Texas A&M University.

tion of Borlaug's scientific and humanitarian contributions relating to the Green Revolution. The $15 million Borlaug Center, funded by the Agricultural Research Service, US Department of Agriculture, provides the Institute for Plant Genomics and Biotechnology with a base of operations including specialized teaching and research laboratories, infrastructure, and equipment for the plant science community at Texas A&M University.

Norman E. Borlaug International Science and Technology Fellows Program

The Norman E. Borlaug International Science and Technology Fellows Program was established in 2003 by the Foreign Agricultural Service, US Department of Agriculture. The Fellowship Program is organized so that the legacy that Dr. Borlaug has created will continue to improve quality of life throughout the world with improved technologies affecting basic food crops. The program helps developing countries adopt and adapt agricultural science and technology. The cornerstone of the program is faculty and scientist exchanges with developing countries, primarily from Africa, Asia, and Latin America. Four US universities joined the program: the University of Minnesota, Texas A&M, Cornell and Iowa State University.

The USDA portion of the program provides short-term scientific training for international agricultural research scientists and policymakers from the developing countries. It provides promising young scientists with opportunities to work with US and international specialists in their fields of agricultural science. During a four-to-six week training period, the selected fellows work closely with their chosen mentor, learn new research techniques, access fully-equipped libraries, and learn about public-private research partnerships. The fellows are trained at US universities, international agricultural research centers, international organizations, and private sector research and policy centers.

The four participating US universities administer longer-term (up to two-year) fellowships for M.S. and Ph.D. candidates. These fellowships are sponsored by the US Agency for International Development. Fellows aspire to Dr. Borlaug's guiding principle: "Food is the moral right of all who are born into this world."

How does Norman Borlaug see himself and all that he has accomplished? In his down-home, unassuming way, he says, "I was only a catalyst."

Chapter Seventeen

Reflections of a Humble Hero of Hunger

"Margaret deserves much, much credit for keeping the family together while I roamed the world for half a century."

—Norman Borlaug

As he enters his 92nd year, a still-active, enthusiastic Norman Borlaug takes time to reflect on his remarkable career. As one might expect, his retrospection reaches back on the Iowa farm. He says:

> I was born and brought up on a small farm in the Midwest in the United States. I am a product of a one-room country school —a modest affair, by all means. That combination of farm and school gave me some insights into the lives of those who had to struggle no end to achieve a higher standard of living. It gave me what I may call a more basic empathy for people of third-world countries.

In a living history interview, Borlaug conveyed early experiences that influenced his philosophy of life: "My interest in world hunger and trying to do something about it dates back to the early 1930s, during the Great Depression. I saw local bank failures in northern Iowa, where I grew up, and I saw many farmers lose their land. I saw their personal property sold by sheriff's sales. The whole country experienced economic disaster. In the fall of 1933, when I enrolled at the University of Minnesota, I was introduced to the unpleasant conditions in a large city—huge numbers of unemployed sleeping on the streets hungry, begging for a nickel to buy food.

"I saw hungry and malnourished young men seventeen or eighteen years old arrive at Civilian Conservation Corps camps, where I worked as a forestry program leader. At the camps, they were able to recover some semblance of health and self-confidence. I saw how food changed them. All of this left scars on me and caused me to want to do something to help."[81]

Norm's chance to "do something to help" came in 1944. "My first foreign assignment was Mexico—a country only next door to the United States of America. Still, the contrast between the two situations was much too apparent.

"Anyway, Mexico at that time, toward the end of the Second World War, had only 22 million mouths to feed. Mexico's population is now 105 million—an increase of nearly five times. At the time that I was working on increasing the output of Mexican wheat and corn, six decades ago, I often would discuss with some of my intimate friends the problem of multiplying mouths, as I was becoming more conscious of the nexus that exists between population, food and the environment. Today, a good number of them complain to me why I did not speak up for curbing population growth when there was still time. But my reply to that is that had I done so, they would have thrown me out, as I was then not so well-recognized by the majority of people."

Soon, another challenging opportunity began to unfold. Norm says, "Little did I imagine then, in the early 1950s, even in my fondest dreams, that the quiet revolution in wheat production in Mexico would become popularly known as the Green Revolution in famine-plagued India and Pakistan, and subsequently spread to many other countries.

"Pakistan became self-sufficient in both wheat and rice production for the first time in 1968, and has remained so up to the present time, despite its large increase in population. India's accomplishments are even more impressive, especially when recalling the widespread famine of 1965 and 1966 which led many authorities to state that India's population had outgrown its food supply and a disastrous 'die-off' of the population was inevitable. India became self-sufficient in wheat in 1972, in all cereals in 1974 and remains so despite population having more than doubled—from approximately 450 million to more than one billion. The larger and more important question now is, how much longer can it remain self-sufficient under the relentless pressure of the human population monster?"

Norman hesitated for a moment as he had a flashback to his childhood and made a nostalgic connection with his adventures in India and Pakistan:

"When I was in the fifth grade in the one-room New Oregon Township #8 in Howard County, Iowa, a teacher, Lena Halvorson, insisted that I memorize among various poems two by Rudyard Kipling: 'If' and 'Gunga Din.' Many times while in Lahore [Pakistan] over the past four decades, I stood beside the plaque and bust that bears Kipling's name and silently recited those two poems. My, how the world has shrunk!"

Dr. Borlaug then talked fondly, yet tempered with a sense of concern, about the set of international agricultural research centers that have contributed so greatly to relieving hunger in developing countries. He said, "The CGIAR centers have undoubtedly played an important role in increasing world food production, but what about their future? The late Dr. F.F. Hill, former vice president of the Ford Foundation and one of the forces behind the creation of the first four international centers and subsequently the CGIAR, told me in 1968 when we were traveling together in Pakistan viewing the tremendous impact of Green Revolution wheat production technology, 'Enjoy it! Such dramatic changes in yield and commercial production are rare, once-in-a-lifetime events.'

"He said he was pleased to see the key role the centers were playing to bring both the wheat and rice revolutions to fruition, but he went on to warn, 'I doubt the centers will have more than twenty-five years of highly productive life before succumbing to the twin ills of bureaucracy and complacency.' If this happened, Dr. Hill thought, it would probably be easier to build a new set of institutions, rather than try to reform the existing ones. I often ask myself, when reflecting on the current problems of the CGIAR, is Dr. Hill's prediction coming true? I hope not, but I must confess I am fearful. We must not let it happen!"

Borlaug is certainly not a disciple of Malthus, but he is concerned by what he calls the "Population Monster." He says, "During my lifetime the world's population has gone from 1.6 billion to 6.4 billion. It is projected to continue to increase before *hopefully* stabilizing at about 10 billion by the end of the twenty-first century. Where will the food come from?"

In answering his own question, he says, "Fortunately, there are still many improved agricultural technologies already available and not being fully used at present—as well as others well advanced in the research pipeline—that can be employed in future years to raise crop yields. There are also large gaps between actual yield and potential yield in virtually all low-income, food-deficit developing nations, as well as in the ex-Soviet Union, Eastern European countries, India, Indonesia, Argentina, Brazil, and sub-Saharan African countries.

"The only way for agriculture to produce sufficient food to keep pace with population and to alleviate hunger is to increase the intensity of agricultural production in those ecological areas which lend themselves to intensification while decreasing the intensity of production in the more fragile ecologies.

"The greatest need now is in sub-Saharan Africa, which faces the horrifying prospect of only producing three-quarters of its food requirements unless fertilizer use is tripled and combined with higher yielding varieties and improved crop management practices."

As we sat reminiscing, Dr. Borlaug said to me, "I believe we agricultural scientists have a moral obligation to warn the political, educational, and religious leaders of the world about the magnitude and seriousness of the arable land, food and population problems that lie ahead. If we fail to do so in a forthright manner, we will be negligent in our duty and inadvertently will be contributing to the pending chaos of incalculable millions of deaths by starvation."

Then he summed up his thinking in one sentence: "Without aggressive agricultural research programs, the world will soon be overwhelmed by the Population Monster."

Norm hesitated a moment before responding to my question, "Dr. Borlaug, what has been your greatest satisfaction in life?"

Following a bit of reflection, he said, "Let me mention just two of the many gratifying moments. One was to see the results of research that produced the technology that initially sparked the 'quiet' wheat revolution in Mexico, where the crop is only of secondary importance to corn, being spread with dramatic impact to large wheat-producing countries, such as India, Pakistan, Egypt, Spain, Italy, Portugal, Argentina, Brazil, China, Australia, Canada, and even the USA, France, Germany and the UK.

"The other comes from my visiting in various countries around the world and seeing the good agricultural research and production being carried out by the many former visiting scientists that we trained in Mexico."

As we sat beside the swimming pool at the CIMMYT campus, each sipping a rum Collins, I asked Norm a question that had been burning inside me for a long time: "Dr. Borlaug, of all the people who have touched your life, who would you say has had the greatest influence?"

Norm took another sip, thought for awhile, and finally said, "You know, that is really difficult for me to say. So many people have done or said things that have made a drastic difference in my life. Margaret, of course, has been an absolute stalwart. She has encouraged me at every step of the way. Without question, she is at the top of the list. She has paid a hefty price for our achievements. She managed the home and kept things together while I was away for months at a time.

"But, to give you an indication why that question is difficult to answer, why I hesitated for a moment, let me name just a few of those who have had a major influence on my life:

"Among the first was my Grandfather Nels Borlaug—and of course Dad and Mother—who throughout my childhood encouraged me to 'get a good education.'

"Then came Dave Bartelma, my wresting coach at Cresco High and later at the University of Minnesota, who taught me to do my best and never give up the struggle to learn and improve.

"Next, if it hadn't been for my buddy George Champlin, I wouldn't have gone to the University of Minnesota; my life's work would have taken an entirely different path.

"Then, there was Dr. Fred Hovde, who arranged for me to transfer from the General College at the University of Minnesota to the School of Agriculture.

"The next influential person was Professor E.C. Stakman, who set me on a path of science and eventually convinced me to join George Harrar's team in Mexico. Aside from Margaret and her unending support and encouragement, I guess I would have to say that Stak had a greater influence on my life than any other single individual. He made me reach for the stars.

"And while Dutch Harrar and I sometimes had different ideas on program tactics, we remained close friends. It was his leadership—his philosophy of giving us a free hand in our search for solutions to Mexico's food problem—that caused it all to happen. From Dutch, I learned how to deal with cabinet members and heads of state. He was a master at dealing with political leaders on sensitive issues.

Borlaug receiving the Edwin Charles Stakman Award, 1961.

"Finally, while I can't pinpoint any one person, the Nobel Selection Committee as a whole, which chose me over all the other worthy competitors in 1970, ultimately made the most drastic change in my life. The Nobel Prize and all that went with it hit me like a typhoon. It threw me into the spotlight so much it made me uncomfortable."

Norm took one last sip on his rum Collins. Then he said, "I often think fondly of those quiet days in isolation on Cold Mountain."

Whatever became of that young man from Little Norway, Iowa, who flunked the entrance exam at the University of Minnesota in 1933? By the summer of 2005, that same young man, now in his 92nd year, had been awarded more than fifty honorary doctorates from institutions in eighteen countries. Those achievements surely bring an alluring smile, like that of the mysterious Mona Lisa, to the lips of Borlaug's muse, the gracious Princess of Serendip.

Epilogue

"For the first time since 1954, the world has a serious threat of a potentially very destructive stem-rust epidemic in wheat—not just in one continent, but probably in Asia, North America and South America, and maybe *in Australia."*

—Norman Borlaug

One of Norman Borlaug's worst fears awakened when he learned that a virulent new strain of stem rust—dubbed Ug99—had emerged in isolated, high-altitude wheat fields in Uganda in 1999. The "shifty, constantly evolving enemy" seemed to disappear for a couple of years. Then, it reemerged in scattered fields in Kenya in 2001 and in Ethiopia in 2003. Borlaug wrote a memorandum to senior scientists in CIMMYT and ICARDA describing the stem-rust situation in East Africa and pointing out its ominous consequences.

Norm says, "Wheat is not a major crop in most of sub-Saharan Africa. In the summer, it is grown only in higher elevations in East Africa, mainly in Ethiopia, some in Kenya and a small amount in Uganda.[82] Even so, uncontrolled rust could cause serious problems in Kenya and especially in Ethiopia, where a million hectares are grown, mostly by small-scale farmers who lack the resources to use chemical control methods. But our *overwhelming fear* is that Ug99 has the pathogenicity to attack a large proportion of the area sown to wheat in Egypt, Turkey, Pakistan, India, Bangladesh, Iran, Iraq, Jordan, Syria, China, the USA, Canada, much of South America and perhaps even Australia."

"Regrettably," Borlaug says, "the wonderful, cooperative, international, world-wide, multi-location testing network that was in place during the 1960 to 1980 period for evaluating experimental wheats against new races of diseases has broken down. Most of the Mexican-trained wheat scientists in the international wheat fraternity have died or retired and a new generation has not been trained to replace them. There has been no serious epidemic of stem rust anywhere in the world since 1954. As a result, administrators, scientists and those who fund science have become complacent. When everything looks fine, they say, 'Why do it?' "

Norman Borlaug was one of the first people that Dr. John Dodds visited when in mid-2004 he took up duties as CIMMYT's new Deputy Director General for Research. Borlaug explained to Dodds that most of CIMMYT's best wheat varieties, and most of the commercial wheat varieties in the world, were probably susceptible to Ug99. Dodds quickly understood the gravity of the situation and told Borlaug that he would look into the problem. His investigation confirmed Borlaug's assessment about the biological threat that Ug99 posed to world wheat production.

Dodds also saw that the international wheat research network that Borlaug had developed in collaboration with more than sixty countries between 1960 and the mid-1980s had essentially fallen apart, due to a combination of complacency and the general malaise that public research has encountered: "Let the private sector do the agricultural research." Budgets for public research had declined. The flow of experimental varieties and research information that Borlaug had championed had fallen prey to legalistic issues of intellectual property rights, fears of bio-terrorism, and plant quarantine restrictions. Gone were the days when an international fraternity of wheat scientists exchanged their most promising experimental wheat varieties in a collegial way. And CIMMYT's international training programs had substantially contracted.

In November 2004, Dodds called Borlaug at his Texas A&M University office: "You know better than I that if this thing gets loose from sub-Saharan Africa, especially in Egypt, it will be very bad. If it should happen to get loose in Asia, it will be catastrophic. I am organizing a meeting of scientists who may be able to help us get on top of the problem. Because of your unique familiarity with rust diseases, we urgently need you to chair the meeting. How soon can you come?"

Borlaug said, "I can be there the first week in January. See if you can assemble the others during that week."

The early January meetings at CIMMYT in Mexico resulted in the outlines of a plan of action to minimize the threat of the rust outbreak in East Africa. Then, Norman Borlaug, Marco Quinones and Chris Dowswell of the Sasakawa Africa Association, after attending a Rockefeller Foundation-sponsored conference in Nairobi, Kenya, in mid-January, traveled with the director of the Kenyan Agricultural Research Institute (KARI) to the high-altitude Njoro Research Station, located near Lake Nakuru and surrounded by high-valley wheat farms, where farmers were struggling to contain Ug99.

Norm says, "A few large wheat farmers, mostly Kenyan farmers of British ancestry, had good wheat. To control rust, they had been spraying with a fungicide for two years. But, hell, rust was everywhere. It was not a killing rust, because it started too late. But next year it will likely start early."

They observed that the small nursery of CIMMYT wheat lines in Kenya was riddled with rust. Borlaug then worked out a plan for international rust nurseries to be established in Kenya and Ethiopia in the summer of 2005. The Rockefeller Foundation pledged $75,000 of seed money; Borlaug pledged $25,000 from the Sasakawa Africa Association.

"In Africa, in the Sasakawa-Global 2000 extension program," Norm says, "we have only six internationally-recruited scientists supported by a larger number—though still small—of national professional staff working in eight countries. They are good people, experienced researchers and extension workers. Our staff in Ethiopia is helping to evaluate large numbers of wheat varieties and breeding lines, including those that were held in cold storage at CIMMYT and ICARDA, and other materials that any country wants to have tested."

Norm says, "This will give a true picture of how bad the situation is."

Borlaug is one of the few living, active scientists with any background on the devastating stem-rust epidemics in the USA and Canada between 1950 and 1954 and the historical development in Mexico of rust-resistant varieties. The Mexican program fostered cooperative spring-wheat testing—two generations per year—with the USA and Canada that grew out of the crisis of the early 1950s. The cooperative program identified new rust-resistant materials and multiplied the seed. Borlaug had carefully catalogued the breeding lines and placed samples of each in the cold storage facilities at CIMMYT. Wheat breeders all over the world started using the resistant lines. "But," Norm says, "a new race of rust will knock them out completely."

Then he expressed some reason for hope, under the assumption that funding for the required work will be forthcoming, "I'm sure there is resistance among the thousands of lines that we placed in cold storage in the early days at CIMMYT, as well as lines in storage in other countries. We need to identify lines of high-yielding dwarf varieties and rapidly multiply the seed of the best lines to replace the susceptible varieties. But, you can't do that in 20 minutes!"

Dr. Borlaug then proclaimed, "For maximum protection from outbreaks of rust disease in the longer run, the world needs to reinstate and maintain the cooperative international world-wide, multi-location testing networks of nurseries to evaluate how experimental new wheats react to various rust races and other diseases. In the absence of such a system, an outbreak of the shifty disease—whether stem rust, leaf rust or stripe rust—could cause havoc and exacerbate much of the world's already serious hunger problem."

African research institutions are now sounding the alarm on the stem-rust problem. An expert panel's report states, "It is only a matter of time before Ug99 reaches across the Saudi Arabian peninsula and into the Middle East, South Asia and, eventually, East Asia and the Americas."[83]

A major meeting of wheat scientists convened in Nairobi, Kenya, on September 9-10, 2005. The day before, to draw attention to the new threat, Dr. Borlaug held a news conference in which he said, "Nobody's seen an epidemic of stem rust for 50 years, nobody in this room except me. Maybe we got too complacent."[84]

Wheat scientists and agricultural policymakers from more than thirty countries gathered to discuss the problems and chart collective actions. Borlaug served as honorary chairman and was a keynote speaker. An objective of the gathering was to begin to rebuild the international wheat system that Borlaug and hundreds of colleagues around the world had so painstakingly constructed 50 years before. Still to be determined is whether such a public-goods research system can be constructed under today's conditions of globalization and fears of international bio-terrorism.

But Borlaug is optimistic. "Rusts recognize no political boundaries. To control rust pandemics, there is no alternative to international cooperation. Cooperation, not competition, must be the order of the day."

Acknowledgments

First and foremost, I owe a debt of gratitude to the prime subject of this book, Norman Borlaug, for the many, many hours we spent together discussing topics dear to his heart, including issues surrounding his chief concern: How can the world continue to feed its growing populations and maintain peace? I marvel at his insights, curiosity, and common sense as he wrestles with these and other important events.

I owe special thanks to the following people who have known and worked with Dr. Borlaug off and on for the past several decades, who graciously read earlier drafts of the manuscript, gave advice, and suggested improvements. Among these are George McGovern, Lowell Hardin, Eugene Hayden, Ed Runge, Christopher Dowswell, Guy Baird, William Hueg, and Vernon Ruttan.

Others who reviewed selected chapters and made helpful suggestions include Miki Hayden, David Fryxell, Joyce McDonald, Diana Oleskow, Ruth Pattrin, Betty Barry, Barbara Scott, Deanie Blank, George Kotlan, Patti Lyons, Jin Robertson, Tori Hamilton, Tara DeDecker, Vanessa Atler, Ellen Taliaferro, Harvey Webb, Vera Stern, and Eleanor Wolf.

Ilihia Gionson, a bright, young, up-and-coming Hawaiian author whom I met at the 2005 writers' retreat in Maui, after a few days' exposure to the subject, suggested the title, *The Man Who Fed the World.* Thank you, Ilihia.

About the Author

Leon Hesser's service as a teenage soldier in the Philippines during World War II, and later with the Army of Occupation in Japan, exposed him to cultures and farming systems that differed from those he had grown up with in the Midwest of the United States. The differences fascinated him.

After the war, Hesser married Florence Ellen Life, they had two children, and they farmed in Indiana until he was 30, when his city-bred wife encouraged him to sell the farm business and enter Purdue University as a freshman. He earned bachelor's, master's, and Ph.D. degrees in agricultural economics at Purdue, with emphasis on international agriculture.

In 1966, Hesser joined the Foreign Service and went to Pakistan, where he headed the US government's technical assistance program to increase food production in that country, where hunger was widespread. He and his team helped Dr. Norman Borlaug, a Rockefeller Foundation scientist, introduce Borlaug's high-yielding wheat seeds and production technology. Wheat production doubled in four years.

After seven years in Pakistan, Dr. Hesser was assigned to Washington, DC, where he was director of worldwide programs to increase food production in developing nations. In that capacity, he and his staff managed the US government's financial input to the set of fifteen international agricultural research centers that are fundamental to increasing global food production.

Hesser retired from the Foreign Service in 1978 and worked another 22 years as a consultant to increase food production in twenty countries of Africa, Asia and more recently in Russia and Ukraine, where he helped transform collective farms to private ownership by the workers on the farms.

Appendix A

Norman Ernest Borlaug's Ancestral Heritage[85]

The Borlaug Ancestors

On April 4, 1854, Ole Olson Dybevig and his wife Solveig Thomasdaughter Rinde immigrated to America from Norway. They hailed from Feios, Norway, near the Borlaug settlement on Sognefjord. Because they came from a farm area by that name, they took Borlaug as their last name.

Immigrants usually had very little money. Part of the spirit of the frontier was that immigrants would initially buy a small piece of land from a family that had moved to a larger piece. Ole and Solveig Borlaug settled first on a small farm near Green Bay, Wisconsin, where their first two sons—Ole and Thomas—were born. Shortly, they moved to a slightly larger farm near Norway Grove, Wisconsin, where Norman's granddad Nels was born.[86] As early as 1847, Norway Grove, Dane County, Wisconsin, was a popular destination for immigrants from Norway.

Norman Borlaug's great-grandfather Ole Olson Dybevig was born in Dybevig, Leikanger, Sogn, Norway on March 29, 1821. He was the son of Ole Olson Indre Dybevig and Anna Bottolfsdatter, who were married in an area known as Borlaug, Norway, on November 2, 1820.[87]

On March 26, 1854, in Feioskyrkje i Rinde, Balestrand, Sogn, great-grandfather Ole married Solveig Thomasdaughter Rinde (daughter of Thomas Rinde and Martha Fosshage) who was born November 22, 1831, in Feios, Leikanger, Sogn, Norway.

The Dybevig-Rinde-Borlaug farms were alongside Sognefjord (Sogn Fjord) in the Leikanger Church community in Norway.

Ole and Solveig Borlaug lived in Wisconsin about five years.

Their children were Ole, Thomas, Nels (Norman's grandfather), born in Wisconsin; Anna, born in South Dakota; and Johan, born in Iowa.

Norman Borlaug's grandfather Nels Olson Borlaug was born October 25, 1859, at Norway Grove, Wisconsin. Just a few weeks after Nels was born, the family went west with a group of other Norwegian-American families by covered wagon to the Vermillion, South Dakota area, on the banks of the Missouri River, where they lived about three years.

There was much unrest for the new settlers, partly because of the Civil War and partly due to uncertainty caused by Sioux Indian massacres at Spirit Lake, Iowa, and New Ulm, Minnesota, in which a number of people were killed. To avoid being scalped, the Borlaugs and other residents hitched their oxen to 13 wagons, headed back east and settled in northeastern Iowa. Two of the families settled at Cedar Falls, Iowa; nine of the families settled at Jerico, Iowa, in an area known as the Little Turkey Settlement. The Ole Borlaug family lived near Calmar, Iowa, for one year and then moved to the Little Turkey Settlement, two miles north of Saude, Iowa, where they dropped anchor.

The hardships that those families endured included hard, cold winters; wet and muddy trails; and un-bridged rivers to cross. To cross the rivers, they cut trees for logs, tied them to the sides of their wagons and floated across, propelled by the swimming oxen.

The Vaala, Landsverk, and Swenumson Families

Agriculture and forestry were the most important occupations in the Norwegian community of Saude (this was a Danish name that in 1928 was changed back to Sauherad, the original Norwegian name). As population increased, the number of farms and smallholdings increased almost threefold from 1730 to 1865; this led to the partitioning of farms and new areas being cleared for cultivation in the nineteenth century. The situation was exacerbated by the mid-nineteenth century potato famine in Europe, caused by the late-blight fungus. "Lefsa," a popular staple (tortilla-like) food made from potatoes, was threatened by the potato famine. Many Saude citizens immigrated to America in search of a better future.

Among them were the Vaala, Landsverk, and Swenumson families, who sailed from Saude, Telemark County, Norway, to America on the same ship in 1848. All three families settled in northeastern Iowa and named their community Saude.

The Vaala, Landsverk, and Swenumson families had attended the Roman-style, twelfth century church in Saude (Sauherad). The church's four-foot-thick walls are made of rough-hewn granite. Toward the rear of the church is a small weapon room. In the early days, many "small kings" fought for power and occasionally the church members had to defend themselves.

The Families Intermarry

On June 16, 1885, Nels Borlaug married Emma Swenumson, who was born August 12, 1864 in Iowa. Nels and Emma had four children: Oscar Simon, born May 8, 1886 (never married); Norman's father, Henry Oliver, born April 12, 1889; Ned Elmer, born April 17, 1895; and Clara Murial (Cochran[88]), born May 20, 1900.

Ole Vaala married Kari Landsverk. Their daughter Clara was born September 28, 1888.

Henry Oliver Borlaug was born near Saude, in New Oregon Twp., Howard County, Iowa. In Saude on August 14, 1913, he married Clara Vaala, who was born September 28, 1888. Henry and Clara had four children: Norman Ernest, born March 25, 1914; Palma Lillian, born on Palm Sunday, 1916; Charlotte, born August 28, 1919; and Helen, who was born and died in April 1921.

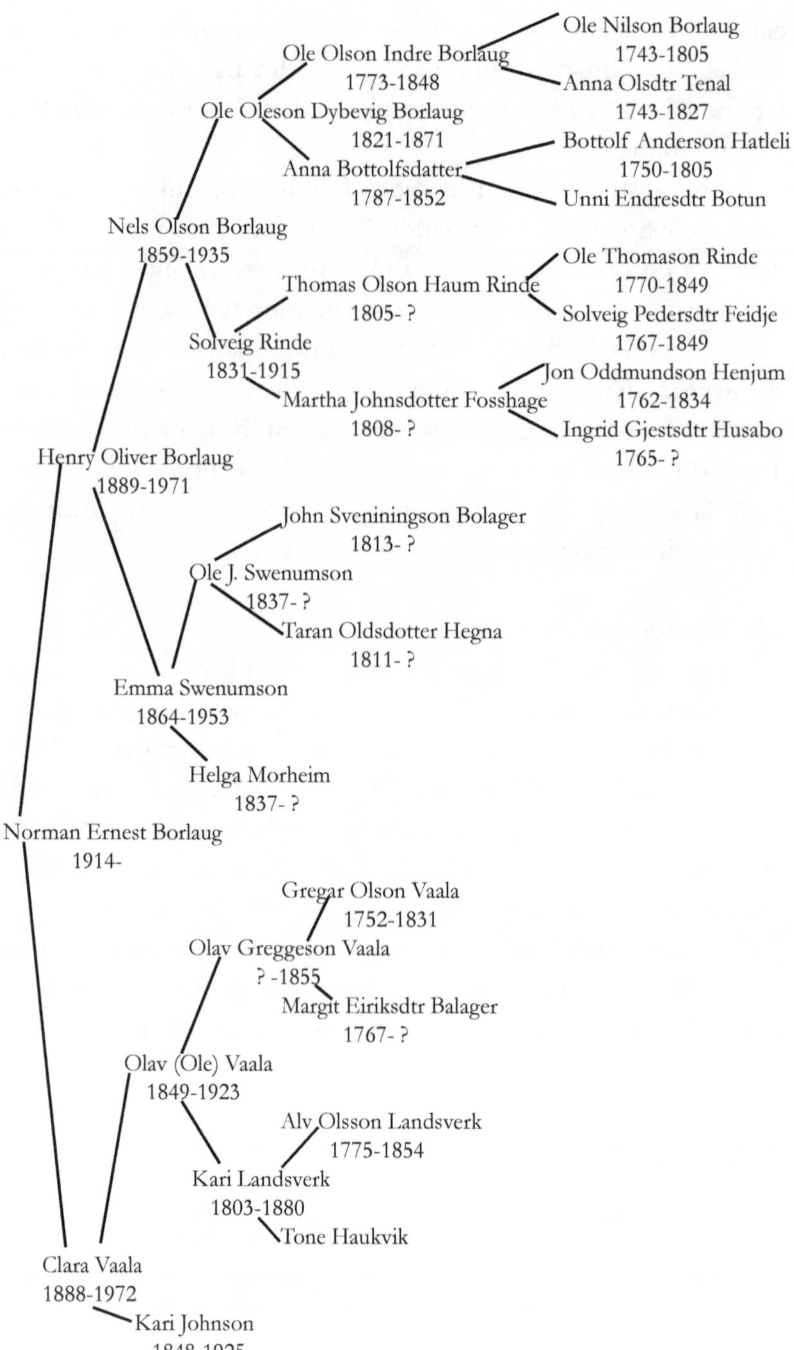
Ole Nilson Borlaug
1743-1805
Ole Olson Indre Borlaug
1773-1848
Anna Olsdtr Tenal
1743-1827
Ole Oleson Dybevig Borlaug
1821-1871
Bottolf Anderson Hatleli
1750-1805
Anna Bottolfsdatter
1787-1852
Unni Endresdtr Botun
Nels Olson Borlaug
1859-1935
Ole Thomason Rinde
1770-1849
Thomas Olson Haum Rinde
1805- ?
Solveig Pedersdtr Feidje
1767-1849
Solveig Rinde
1831-1915
Jon Oddmundson Henjum
1762-1834
Martha Johnsdotter Fosshage
1808- ?
Ingrid Gjestsdtr Husabo
1765- ?
Henry Oliver Borlaug
1889-1971
John Sveniningson Bolager
1813- ?
Ole J. Swenumson
1837- ?
Taran Oldsdotter Hegna
1811- ?
Emma Swenumson
1864-1953
Helga Morheim
1837- ?
Norman Ernest Borlaug
1914-
Gregar Olson Vaala
1752-1831
Olav Greggeson Vaala
? -1855
Margit Eiriksdtr Balager
1767- ?
Olav (Ole) Vaala
1849-1923
Alv Olsson Landsverk
1775-1854
Kari Landsverk
1803-1880
Tone Haukvik
Clara Vaala
1888-1972
Kari Johnson
1848-1925

Appendix B

Awards Received by Norman Borlaug

In addition to the coveted Nobel Peace Prize, following is a partial list of the many academic, scientific and achievement awards that have been bestowed upon Dr. Norman E. Borlaug:

- Outstanding Achievement Award — 1959
  University of Minnesota

- The Edwin Charles Stakman Award — 1961
  University of Minnesota

- Founding Member Award — 1964
  Instituto Nacional de Investigaciones Agricolas (Mexico)

- Recognition Award — 1966
  Agricultural Institute of Canada

- Cuidad Obregon named a street Norman Borlaug[89] — 1968

- National Academy of Sciences of USA — 1968

- *Sitara-i-Imtiaz* (The Star of Distinction) — 1968
  President Ayub Khan of Pakistan

- Recognition Award (Argentina) — 1968
  Instituto Nacional de Tecnologia Agropecuaria de Marcos Juarez

- Honorary Fellow 1968
  India Society of Genetics and Plant Breeding

- First International Service Award in Agronomy 1968
  American Society of Agronomy

- Meritorius Service Award and Honorary Life Membership 1969
  American Association of Cereal Chemists

- Uncle of Paul Bunyan (Forestry) 1969
  University of Minnesota

- Aztec Eagle, Government of Mexico 1970

- Scientific Service Award 1970
  El Colegio de Ingenieros Agronomos de Mexico

- Diploma de Merito 1971
  El Instituto Tecnologico y de Estudios Superiores de Monterrey

- Honorary Foreign Academician of N.I. 1971
  Vavilov Academy of Agricultural Sciences (USSR)

- Foreign Member, The Royal Swedish Academy of Agriculture and Forestry 1971

- Medalla y Diploma de Merito "Antonio Narro" 1971
  de la Escuela Superior de Agricultura de la Universidad de Coahuila

- Diploma as Distinguished Geneticist 1971
  Sociedad Mexicana de Fitogenetica

- First Honorary Life Membership 1971
  American Society of Agronomy, Crop Science

- Honorary Member 1971
  Sociedad de Agronomia do Rio Grande do Sul (Brazil)

- Merit Award 1971
  Associacao dos Engenheiros Agronomos do Distrito Federal do Brazil

- Recognition Award 1971
  Punjab Agricultural Research Institute (Pakistan)

- Medal, Consultor Emeritos 1971
  Instituto Nacional de Tecnologia Agropecuaria (Argentina)

- Outstanding Achievement Award 1971
  University of Minnesota "M" (Athletic) Club

- Diploma de Merito 1973
  Escuela Superior de Agricultura Hermanos Escobar (Mexico)

- Centennial Foreign Fellow 1976
  American Chemical Society

- The Presidential Medal of Freedom 1977
  United States of America

- First Honorary Life Membership 1978
  Bangladesh Botanical Society

- First Honorary Membership 1978
  Bangladesh Association for the Advancement of Science

- Jefferson Award 1980
  American Institute for Public Service

- Agricultural Hall of Fame and Distinguished Service Award 1981
  Oregon State University

- Honorary Member 1981
  Japan Society for Promotion of Science

- Honorary Citizen of the State of Sonora, Mexico 1983

- The Henry G. Bennett Distinguished Service Award 1984
  Oklahoma State University

- Fellow 1985
  Crop Science Society of America

- Certificate of Outstanding Achievement 1985
  President Ronald Reagan

- Foreign Member, Royal Society (London) 1987

- National Wrestling Hall of Fame (USA) 1992

- University of Minnesota Athletic Hall of Fame 1994

- The Big Ten (Athletic) Conference Centennial 1995
  Scholar Athletic Medal

- Presidential Award 1997
  Crop Science Society of America

- Honorary Professor 1999
  China Agricultural University

- Honorary Member 1999
  Ingenieros Agronomos del Centro y Canarias (Spain)

- National Award for Service to American and World Agriculture 1999
  National Association of County Agricultural Agents

- Mazorca de Oro (Golden Ear of Maize) 1999
  Escuela Nacional de Agricultura Roberto Quinones
  El Salvador

- Vannevar Bush Award 2000
  National Science Board of the United States

- Distinguished Achievement Award 2001
  American Council on Science and Health

- Public Welfare Medal 2002
  National Academy of Sciences of the United States

- The Philip Hauge Abelson Prize 2002
  American Association for the Advancement of Science

- John P. McGovern Science and Society Award 2003
  Sigma Xi

- Award for Distinguished Achievements to Science & Medicine 2003
  American Council of Science and Health

- Fila Lifetime Achievement Award 2003
  New York Athletic Club

- The President's National Medal of Science 2004
  United States of America

- The Charles A. Black Award — 2005
  The Council for Agricultural Science and Technology

- Padma Vibhushan — 2006
  Government of India

- Congressional Gold Medal — 2007
  United States of America

Honorary Doctorates

Between 1968 and 2006, 55 honorary doctorates were conferred on Norman Borlaug by institutions in 18 countries (Argentina, Bangladesh, Bolivia, Chile, Dominican Republic, Germany, Ghana, Hungary, India, Italy, Japan, Norway, Pakistan, The Philippines, Poland, United Kingdom, USA, and Spain).

Honorary Memberships in Academies of Science

Norman Borlaug is a foreign member of academies of science in Argentina, Bangladesh, China, Hungary, India, Mexico, Norway, Pakistan, Poland, Rumania, Russia (then USSR), Sweden, and United Kingdom.

Notes

[1] See Appendix A for a summary history of Norman Borlaug's ancestors.

[2] Topping, *The Hovde Years* (p 91)

[3] Topping (p 94)

[4] Paul Dienhart, *Update*, 1986

[5] The Rockefeller Foundation was established by John D. Rockefeller, Sr., in 1913 "to promote the well-being of mankind throughout the world."

[6] *The Life of Henry A. Wallace: 1888-1965* (website: Henry A. Wallace—Biography)

[7] Graham White and John Maze, *Henry A. Wallace: His Search for a New World Order*. Chapel Hill: University of North Carolina Press, 1995 (p 14)

[8] *American Dreamer*

[9] Stakman, et. al., *Campaigns against Hunger*

[10] Stakman, et. al., *Campaigns against Hunger*

[11] The Marshall Plan to restore Europe was launched in 1948; President Truman's Point Four program to improve agriculture in developing countries was started seven years after The Rockefeller Foundation's program in Mexico.

[12] John J. McKelvey, Jr., "J. George Harrar–December 2, 1906–April 18, 1982," p 32-33

[13] J. George Harrar, *Strategy Toward the Conquest of Hunger*, 1967 (p 202)

[14] Much of the remainder of this chapter is abstracted from four documents: Borlaug's 1970 Nobel lecture; an address by Robert Herdt at Texas A&M in 1998; Harrar's *Strategy Toward the Conquest of Hunger;* and Bickel's *Facing Starvation*

[15] Stakman, et. al., pgs 74-75

[16] Bickel, 120

[17] Bickel, 136

[18] CIMMYT. 1987. *The Future Development of Maize and Wheat in the Third World.* El Batan, Mexico: CIMMYT

[19] Don Paarlberg, page 13

[20] Stakman, et. al, page 81

[21] Borlaug letter to Paul Peterson, May 3, 2000

[22] In 1960, the name was changed to Crop Quality Council.

[23] Harrar, pgs 7-8

[24] Stakman, et. al, *Campaigns against Hunger*, page 90

[25] Stakman, et. al, page 177

[26] *American Dreamer,* page 418

[27] *American Dreamer,* page 251

[28] The FAO trip is described in Dil, p 493

[29] Borlaug's Memoirs, Chp 27, p 7

[30]Herdt's address given at Texas A&M

[31] Lowell S. Hardin, *Memoir,* p 92.

[32] Lowell S. Hardin, *Memoir,* p 104

[33] Herdt

[34] Paddock, *Famine 1975!*

[35] Ehrlich, *The Population Bomb,* page 36

[36] Harrar, *Strategy Toward the Conquest of Hunger,* p 306

[37] Borlaug and Aresvik (1970)

[38] The story of India's "wheat revolution" is adapted partly from Dr. Borlaug's keynote lecture at the International Symposium on Challenges for Global Food and Fibre Production, arranged by The Royal Swedish Academy of Agriculture and Forestry at Folkets Hus, Stockholm, January 27, 1988, which was published in *The Journal of The Royal Swedish Academy of Agriculture and Forestry,* Supplement 21, PP. 15-55, 1988, and reprinted in Anwar Dil, *Norman Borlaug on World Hunger,* 1997

[39] Borlaug, Keynote Lecture at the International Symposium, Stockholm, January 27, 1988

[40] Hesser, *Nurture the Heart, Feed the World*, page 18

[41] CIMMYT. 1987. *The Future Development of Maize and Wheat in the Third World.* El Batan, Mexico: CIMMYT

[42] Gaud, William S., Administrator, Agency for International Development, Department of State. "The Green Revolution: Accomplishments and Apprehensions," Address before The Society for International Development, Shoreham Hotel, Washington, DC, March 8, 1968

[43] CIMMYT. 1987. *The Future Development of Maize and Wheat…*

[44] Edwin J. Wellhausen, in the foreword to the book, *Norman Borlaug on World Hunger*, edited by Dr. Anwar Dil. San Diego: Bookservice International, 1997

[45] Chandler, pgs 4 & 5

[46] Harrar, p 252

[47] Baum, p 17

[48] Baum, p 28

[49] Baum, pgs 28-29

[50] Baum, p 30

[51] Lowell S. Hardin, *Memoir*, p 91

[52] Baum, p 65

[53] Lowell S. Hardin, *Memoir*, p 91

[54] Lowell S. Hardin, *Memoir*, p 93

[55] Borlaug, "Challenges for Global Food and Fiber Production," Keynote Lecture on Challenges for Global Food and Fibre Production, arranged by The Royal Swedish Academy of Agriculture and Forestry at Folkets Hus, Stockholm, January 27, 1988. (Reprinted in Anwar Dil, p 273)

[56] Dil, "Prologue"

[57] Wortman, p 205

[58] Baum, pgs 236-237

[59] Borlaug in collaboration with Christopher R. Dowswell, "The Importance of Agriculture and a Stable Adequate Food Supply to the Well-Being of Humankind," paper presented at Harvard University, 1995 (Reprinted in Anwar Dil, p 403)

[60] Borlaug, "Agricultural Production: Impact and Challenges," 1995

[61] Borlaug, "Sustainable Agriculture: For How Many, at What

Standard of Living, and Over What Period of Time?" presented at the International Symposium on Sustainable Development, at The World Trade Center, Taipei, Taiwan, sponsored by Texas A&M University, USA, and the Industrial Technology Research Institute, Taiwan, June 5-7, 1995. (Reprinted in Anwar Dil, p 431)

62 Robert W. Herdt, "The Life and Work of Norman Borlaug, Nobel Laureate," lecture at Texas A&M University, January 14, 1998

63 Following Ryoichi Sasakawa's death, the name was changed to Nippon Foundation of Japan.

64 Borlaug, "The Green Revolution: Past Successes and Future Challenges," address at the 34th Convocation of the Indian Agricultural Research Institute, New Delhi, February 9, 1996. (Reprinted in Anwar Dil, p 449)

65 Borlaug article, "We can feed the world; here's how," in the *Wall Street Journal* on May 13, 2002

66 Harry Dunphy, Associated Press article, June 2, 2005

67 "Africa Could Feed Itself," *New York Times,* December 3, 2002

68 L. Hardin (Rome, 1998)

69 Borlaug, "Agricultural Production: Impact and Challenges," presented to CGIAR in Lucerne, February 9, 1995

70 Scott Standley in *Great Decisions*, 2005 Edition, page 79

71 Standley, page 73

72 Easterbrook, The Atlantic Monthly, 1997

73 Harrington, Jerome F. and Bill W. Sorenson, *Development of Brazilian Campo Cerrado Lands—IRI's Experience,* Misc. Pub # 6, IRI Research Institute (2004)

74 Fedoroff and Brown, *Mendel in the Kitchen* (2004)

75 Fedoroff and Brown, *Mendel in the Kitchen* (2004)

76 Kym Anderson, et al (August 2004)

77 Avery & Avery, Hudson Institute (November 2004)

78 National Academy of Sciences, "Safety of Genetically Engineered Foods: Approaches to Assessing Unintended Health

Effects," 2004

[79] St. Louis *Post-Dispatch*, December 5, 2004

[80] Borlaug, "Challenges for Global Food and Fiber Production," Stockholm, January 27, 1988

[81] "Living History Interview," The University of Iowa, October 1991

[82] During the winter season, wheat is grown further south, especially in Zimbabwe and the Republic of South Africa.

[83] CIMMYT, "Sounding the Alarm on Global Stem Rust: An Assessment of Race Ug99 in Kenya and Ethiopia and the Potential for Impact in Neighboring Regions and Beyond," May 29, 2005

[84] *The New York Times*, "New Strain of Wheat Rust Appears in Africa," September 9, 2005.

[85] Data for this appendix were abstracted from pieces supplied to the author by various relatives of Norman Borlaug. Prominent among these was one supplied by John L. Vaala, "The Vaala Family Genealogy, 1638 through 2004,"and one supplied by Norman's cousin Alan Borlaug, "Family Line Dal (or Dahl) from about 570 A.D."

[86] On April 4, 1854, sheriff Johan-Heiberg Landmark signed an emigration certificate for Ole Olson Dybevig with his wife Solveig Thomasdotter. The certificate indicated that Ole was 33 years old, had blue eyes and brown hair, and that there were no communicable diseases in the Sogn area.

[87] Ole Olsen Dybevig's ancestors were of Norwegian nobility, the Dahl family, which was prominent in medieval times. A branch of the old Norwegian royal family goes back to Harold the Fair-Haired (the first King of Norway). The recent King Olav V is of the same family, which can be traced to 900 AD.

[88] Douglas and Clara Borlaug Cochran had two sons, Oliver and Donald, and a daughter, Elna. Donald became an outstanding entomologist who spent his entire carrier as a professor and head of the Department of Entomology at VPI.

[89] To honor Dr. Borlaug, citizens of the State of Sonora and the City and Rotary Club of Cuidad Obregon named a street *Norman Borlaug*. The street runs from the city to Ciano Agricultural Research Center. Dr. Borlaug says, "This I consider one of my greatest honors. It came from the people I had served since 1945, who provided my program enthusiastically with both psychological and economic support."

Bibliography

Anderson, Kym; Lee Ann Jackson and Chantal Pohl Nielsen. "Genetically Modified Rice Adoption: Implications for Welfare and Poverty Alleviation," World Bank Policy Research Working Paper 3380, August 2004.

Baum, Warren C. *Partners Against Hunger: The Consultative Group on International Agricultural Research*. Washington, DC: The World Bank, 1986.

Bickel, Lennard. *Facing Starvation: Norman Borlaug and the Fight Against Hunger*. Readers' Digest Press, 1974.

Borlaug, Norman E., "Agricultural Production: Impact and Challenges," presented at the Consultative Group for International Research (CGIAR) Ministerial-Level Meeting held at Lucerne, Switzerland, February 9, 1995.

______, "Announcement of the 1988 World Food Prize to Dr. Robert F. Chandler, Jr. of USA," remarks at a press conference on June 7, 1988.

______, "Announcement of the 1989 World Food Prize to Dr. Verghese Kurien of India," remarks at a news conference at the National Press Club, June 6, 1989.

______, "Announcement of the 1993 World Food Prize to Dr. He Kang of The People's Republic of China," remarks at a news conference at the National Press Club, Washington, DC, October 14, 1993.

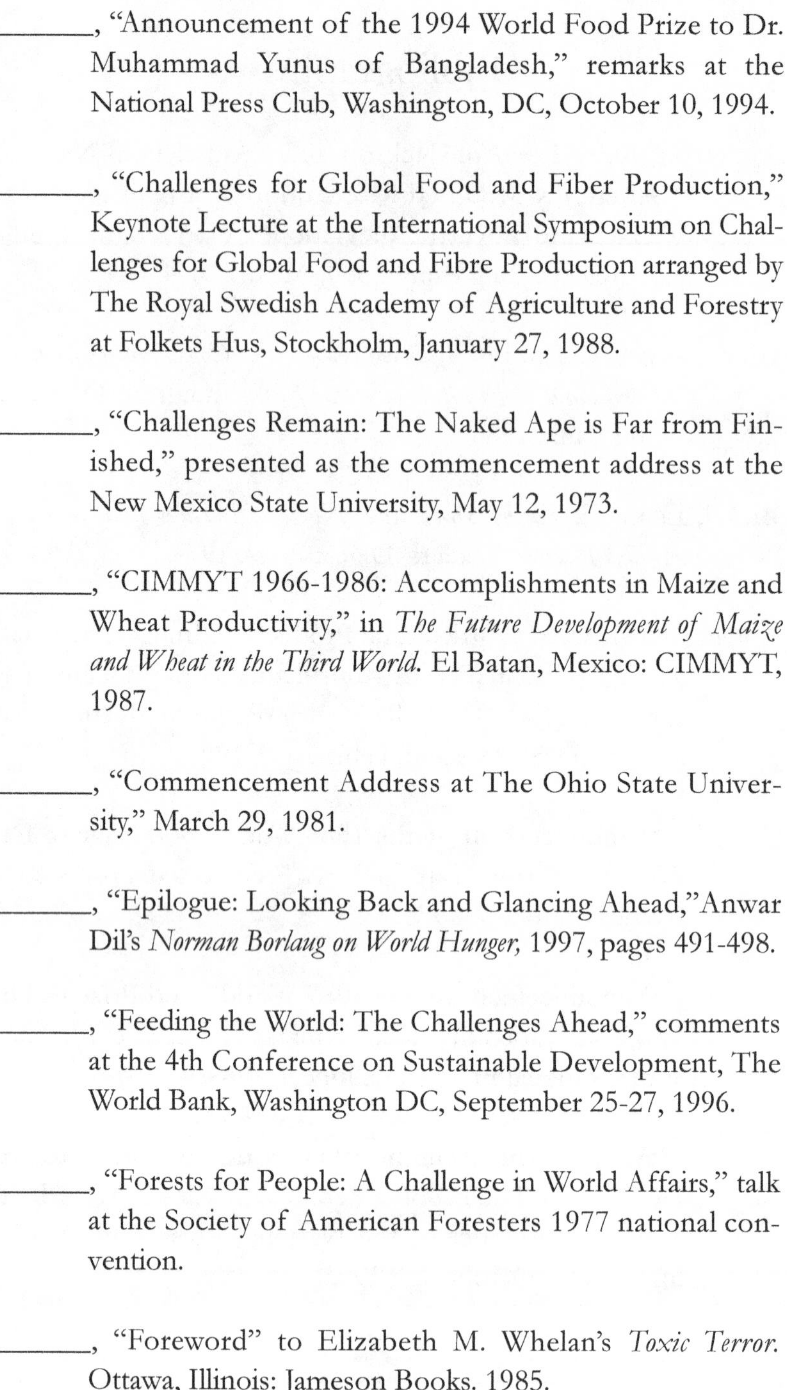

______, "Announcement of the 1994 World Food Prize to Dr. Muhammad Yunus of Bangladesh," remarks at the National Press Club, Washington, DC, October 10, 1994.

______, "Challenges for Global Food and Fiber Production," Keynote Lecture at the International Symposium on Challenges for Global Food and Fibre Production arranged by The Royal Swedish Academy of Agriculture and Forestry at Folkets Hus, Stockholm, January 27, 1988.

______, "Challenges Remain: The Naked Ape is Far from Finished," presented as the commencement address at the New Mexico State University, May 12, 1973.

______, "CIMMYT 1966-1986: Accomplishments in Maize and Wheat Productivity," in *The Future Development of Maize and Wheat in the Third World.* El Batan, Mexico: CIMMYT, 1987.

______, "Commencement Address at The Ohio State University," March 29, 1981.

______, "Epilogue: Looking Back and Glancing Ahead,"Anwar Dil's *Norman Borlaug on World Hunger,* 1997, pages 491-498.

______, "Feeding the World: The Challenges Ahead," comments at the 4th Conference on Sustainable Development, The World Bank, Washington DC, September 25-27, 1996.

______, "Forests for People: A Challenge in World Affairs," talk at the Society of American Foresters 1977 national convention.

______, "Foreword" to Elizabeth M. Whelan's *Toxic Terror.* Ottawa, Illinois: Jameson Books. 1985.

______, "Human Population, Food Demands, and Wildlife Needs," address to the Thirty-Seventh North American Wildlife Conference, 1971.

______, "Humankind and Civilization at Another Crossroad," 1971 McDougall Lecture, November 8, 1971.

______, "Japan's Contribution to the Development of the Green Revolution Semidwarf Wheat Varieties," presented at the memorial ceremony for the Japanese scientist Gongiro Inazuka, June 1, 1990, Johana, Japan.

______, "My Concerns about America are Much Broader than Agriculture and Food," presented at the American Society of Agronomy Convention, San Antonio, Texas, October 23, 1990.

______, "Nobel Lecture: The Green Revolution, Peace and Humanity," delivered at Oslo, Norway, December 11, 1970.

______, "Overview of the Global 2000 Agricultural Projects in Africa," presented at the 1989 workshop on Feeding the Future: Agricultural Development Strategies for Africa, Center for Applied Studies in International Negotiations /Sasakawa Africa Association /Global 2000, August 1-3, 1989.

______, "Population: A Challenge to Contemporary Development Strategies," presented as the inaugural address in the Encounter-with-Population-Crisis lecture series sponsored by the Family Planning Foundation, New Delhi, India, March 11, 1990.

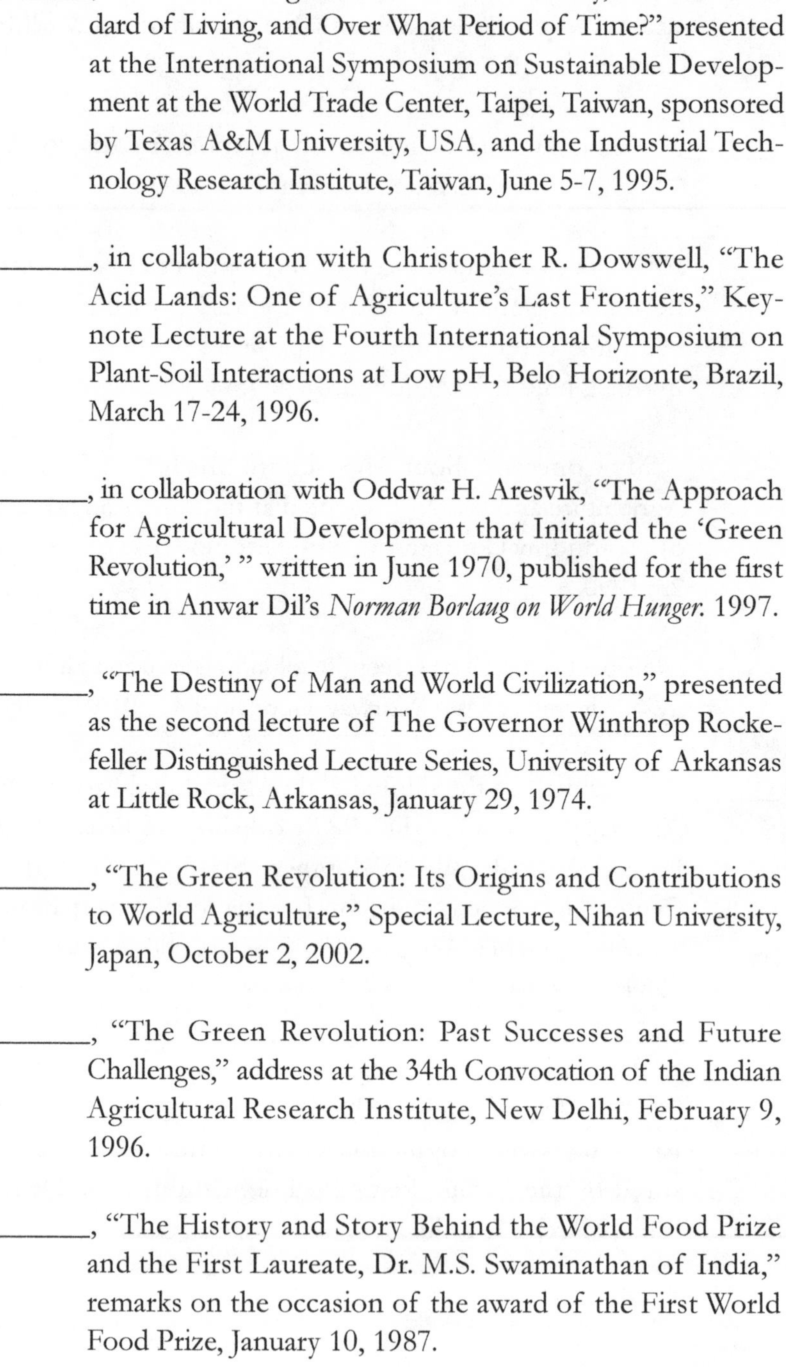

______, "Sustainable Agriculture: For How Many, at What Standard of Living, and Over What Period of Time?" presented at the International Symposium on Sustainable Development at the World Trade Center, Taipei, Taiwan, sponsored by Texas A&M University, USA, and the Industrial Technology Research Institute, Taiwan, June 5-7, 1995.

______, in collaboration with Christopher R. Dowswell, "The Acid Lands: One of Agriculture's Last Frontiers," Keynote Lecture at the Fourth International Symposium on Plant-Soil Interactions at Low pH, Belo Horizonte, Brazil, March 17-24, 1996.

______, in collaboration with Oddvar H. Aresvik, "The Approach for Agricultural Development that Initiated the 'Green Revolution,' " written in June 1970, published for the first time in Anwar Dil's *Norman Borlaug on World Hunger.* 1997.

______, "The Destiny of Man and World Civilization," presented as the second lecture of The Governor Winthrop Rockefeller Distinguished Lecture Series, University of Arkansas at Little Rock, Arkansas, January 29, 1974.

______, "The Green Revolution: Its Origins and Contributions to World Agriculture," Special Lecture, Nihan University, Japan, October 2, 2002.

______, "The Green Revolution: Past Successes and Future Challenges," address at the 34th Convocation of the Indian Agricultural Research Institute, New Delhi, February 9, 1996.

______, "The History and Story Behind the World Food Prize and the First Laureate, Dr. M.S. Swaminathan of India," remarks on the occasion of the award of the First World Food Prize, January 10, 1987.

______, R. Glenn Anderson and Ernest W. Sprague, *The Human Population Monster*, CIMMYT (3 pages). 1980.

______, "The Impact of Agricultural Research on Mexican Wheat Production." Reprinted from *Transactions of the New York Academy of Sciences*, January 1958.

______, in collaboration with Christopher R. Dowswell, "The Importance of Agriculture and a Stable Adequate Food Supply to the Well-Being of Humankind," paper presented at Harvard University, 1995.

______, "The Potential Impact of Quality Maize at the Global Level," presented at the International Symposium on Quality Protein Maize Improvement and Use, Sete Lagoas, MG, Brazil, December 1-3, 1994.

______, "The World Food Problem—Present and Future," presented at the 1971 Nobel Conference organized by the Gustavus Adolphus College, St. Peter, Minnesota.

______, "Wheat Breeding and Its Impact on World Food Supply," Public Lecture at the Third International Wheat Genetics Symposium, Canberra, Australia, August 5-9, 1968.

______, "World Food Security and the Legacy of Canadian Wheat Scientist R. Glenn Anderson," The R. Glenn Anderson Lecture, sponsored jointly by the Canadian Phytopathological Society and the American Phytopathological Society, Grand Rapids, Michigan, August 6, 1990.

______, "Wheat, Rust and People," an invitational address presented at the 56th annual meeting of The American Phytopathological Society, Lafayette, IN. August 24, 1964.

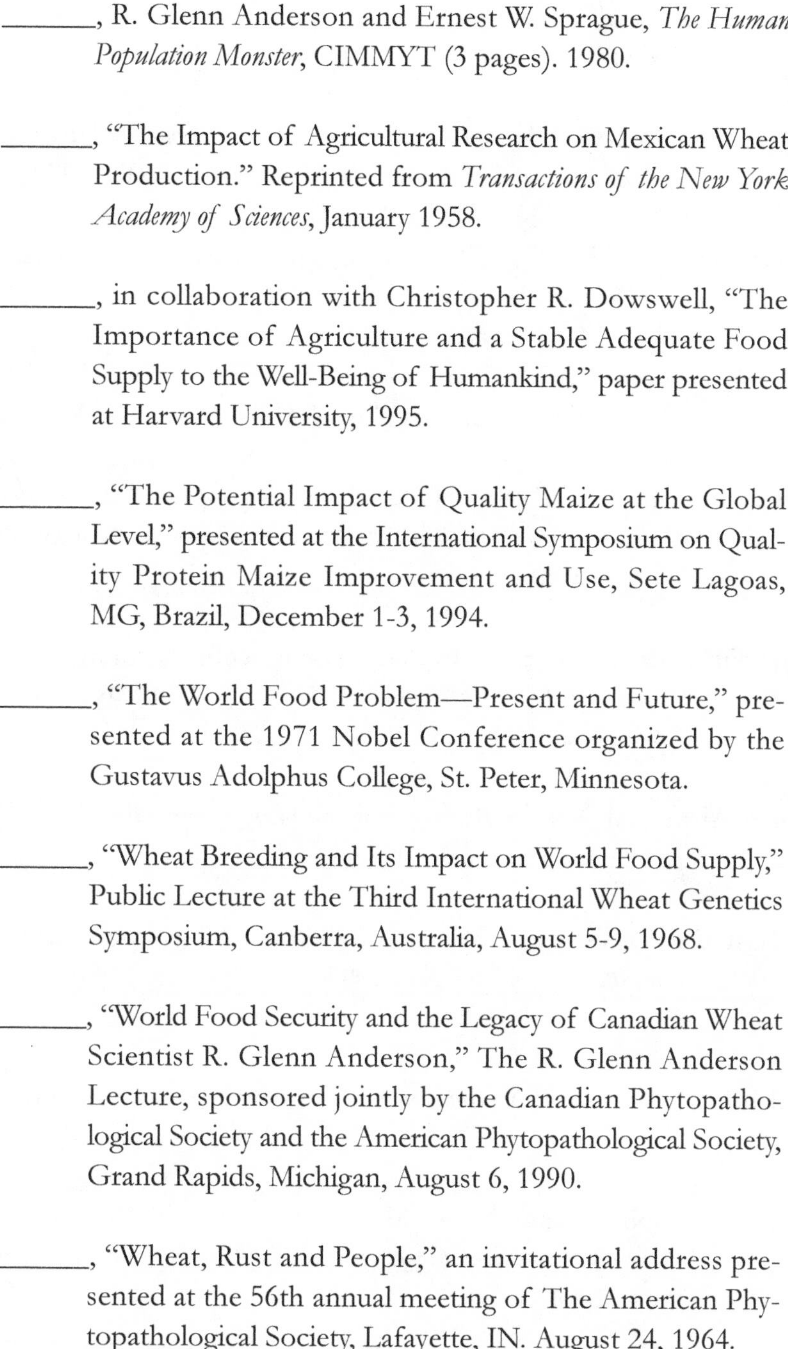

Brown, Lester R. *Seeds of Change: The Green Revolution and Development in the 1970s.* New York: Praeger, 1970.

Chandler, Robert F., Jr. *An Adventure in Applied Science: A History of the International Rice Research Institute.* Manila: IRRI, 1992.

Christensen, C.M. *E.C. Stakman, Statesman of Science.* The American Phytopathological Society, 1984.

Conway, Gordon. *The Doubly Green Revolution: Food for All in the 21st Century.* Ithaca, NY: Cornell University Press, 1999.

Culver, John C. and John Hyde. *American Dreamer: The Life and Times of Henry A. Wallace.* New York: W.W. Norton & Company, 2000.

Dienhart, Paul. "Norman Borlaug: The Peaceful Revolutionary," *Update.* Vol. 13, Number 4, University of Minnesota, April 1986.

Dil, Anwar, ed. *Norman Borlaug on World Hunger.* San Diego: Bookservice International, 1997.

Easterbrook, Gregg. "Forgotten Benefactor of Humanity," *The Atlantic Monthly*, January 1997, Vol. 279, No. 1, pages 75-82.

Ehrlich, Paul. *The Population Bomb.* New York: Ballantine Books, 1968.

Fedoroff, Nina V. and Nancy Marie Brown. *Mendel in the Kitchen: A Scientist's View of Genetically Modified Foods.* Joseph Henry Press, 2004.

Fosdick, Raymond B. *The Story of The Rockefeller Foundation.* New York: Harper & Brothers, 1952.

Freeman, Orville. *World Without Hunger.* New York: Praeger, 1968.

Hanson, Haldore, Norman E. Borlaug and R. Glenn Anderson. *Wheat in the Third World.* Boulder, CO: Westview Press, 1982.

Hardin, Clifford M., ed. *Overcoming World Hunger.* Englewood Cliffs, NJ: Prentice Hall, 1969.

Hardin, Lowell S. "Whence International Agricultural Research," paper delivered at the World Conference on Horticultural Research, Rome, June 17-20, 1998.

Hardin, Lowell S. *Memoir of an International Farmer.* Unpublished, 1999.

Harrar, J. George. *Strategy Toward the Conquest of Hunger.* New York: The Rockefeller Foundation, 1967.

Herdt, Robert W. "The Life and Work of Norman Borlaug, Nobel Laureate," Address at Texas A&M University, January 14, 1998.

Hesser, Leon. *Nurture the Heart, Feed the World.* Austin: Synergy Books, 2004.

Johnson, David Gale. *The Struggle Against World Hunger.* New York: Foreign Policy Association, 1967.

Lionaes, Aase. "Speech to present the Nobel Peace Prize to Norman E. Borlaug," December 10, 1970.

"Living History Interview: Norman Borlaug," *Journal of Law and Contemporary Problems,* College of Law, University of Iowa, October 1991.

McFarland, Martha. "Sowing Seeds of Change," Norman Borlaug Heritage Foundation Resident, 2003.

McGovern, George. *The Third Freedom: Ending Hunger in Our Time.* New York: Rowman & Littlefield Publishers, Inc., 2001.

Miller, Henry I. and Greg Conko. *The Frankenfood Myth: How Protest and Politics Threaten the Biotech Revolution.* Praeger Publishers, 2004.

National Research Council. *Triticale: A Promising Addition to the World's Cereal Grains.* Washington, DC: National Academy Press, 1989.

Paarlberg, Don. *Norman Borlaug: Hunger Fighter.* USG Printing Office, 1970.

________. *Toward a Well-Fed World.* Ames: Iowa State Univ. Press, 1988.

Paddock, William and Paul Paddock. *Famine 1975!: America's Decision; Who Will Survive?* Boston: Little, Brown and Company, 1967.

Pinstrup-Andersen, Per and Ebbe Schioler. *Seeds of Contention: World hunger and the global controversy over GM crops.* Baltimore: Johns Hopkins University Press, 2000.

Ruttan, Vernon W., ed. *Agriculture, Environment & Health: Sustainable development in the 21st century.* Minneapolis: University of Minnesota Press, 1994.

Stakman, E.C., *A Study in Cereal Rusts: Physiological Races.* Minn. Agric. Exp. Sta. Bulletin 138. 1914.

Stakman, E.C. and W.Q. Loegering. *Physiologic races of Puccini graminis in the United States in 1950.* U.S. Dept. Agric.; Bur. Entomol. Plant Quarantine; Bur. Plant Ind., Soils, Agric. Eng.; and Minn. Agric. Exp. Station. 1951.

Stakman, E.C., Richard Bradfield and Paul C. Mangelsdorf. *Campaigns Against Hunger.* Cambridge: Harvard University Press, 1967.

Standley, Scott. "The U.S. and Global Poverty," *Great Decisions,* Foreign Policy Association, 2005 Edition.

Topping, Robert W. *The Hovde Years: A Biography of Frederick L. Hovde.* West Lafayette, Purdue Research Foundation, 1980.

Wellhausen, Edwin J. "Foreword" to Anwar Dil's *Norman Borlaug on World Hunger.* San Diego: Bookservice International, 1997.

White, Graham and John Maze. *Henry A. Wallace: His Search for a New World Order.* Chapel Hill: University of North Carolina Press, 1995.

Wortman, Sterling and Ralph W. Cummings, Jr. *To Feed This World.* Johns Hopkins Press, 1978.

Index

D

E

F

G

H

N

O

P

T

U

Y

Z

CPSIA information can be obtained
at www.ICGtesting.com
Printed in the USA
LVHW090913100820
662127LV00013B/56

9 781948 460101